Designing an Investment Portfolio for American Patriots

Richard Allison

Published by RIA Rules, LLC, 2021.

DESIGNING AN INVESTMENT PORTFOLIO FOR AMERICAN PATRIOTS

First edition. November 9, 2021.

ISBN: 979-8201579029

Written by Richard Allison.

Table of Contents

Dedication

This book is dedicated to your future investment success and more importantly, the future success of America and its people who believe in God and the US Constitution as it was founded.

I would also like to dedicate this book to my extended family. The family members that I know and love today and those who will come after me. Hopefully, one of my descendants will discover this book and learn about me and my view of the world.

Foreword

I have titled my book to focus on American Patriots who believe in God, the founders of this nation, and the US Constitution. It is that simple. This is my belief system, too.

A long time ago, a young man left Scotland as a MacAlister and moved to Northern Ireland to become a farmer. He wanted a new life and a new identity. He changed his last name from MacAlister to Allison. His name was James Cuthbert Allison. His parents gave him his middle name in honor of St. Cuthbert, a Catholic saint who lived centuries earlier in Scotland. James had a son for whom he named John Allison. John Allison had a son named John Allison, Jr., and he had a son named John Allison. The third John Allison came to the British Colonies and settled in Pennsylvania Colony. This John Allison had seven children, one of whom was named William Allison. John the father, Robert, his brother, and William, John's son, all signed the Lancaster Petition on February 6, 1728. You can read a short snippet about it here. https://co.lancaster.pa.us/195/Lancaster-History.

Continuing with our story, William Allison had six children and named one after his father and uncle. His name was John Robert Allison. Apparently, in the mid-1700s, John Robert did not like the Pennsylvania Colony's cold; with his wife Martha (Mattie), they moved south by horse-drawn wagon to Hillsborough, in Orange County, North Carolina. John Robert and his wife Mattie were quite a pair. They had fourteen children! One of those 14 children was Joseph H. Allison, a Lieutenant in the Revolutionary War under Captain William Lytle's Company. Not to be outdone by his father, Joseph H. Allison was married three times and had 17 children! One of those was Joseph Stuart Allison, a General in the North Carolina State Militia after the Revolutionary War. General Allison lived his whole life in Orange County, North Carolina, while his parents and the bulk of his siblings moved to White County, Tennessee.

General Allison had eleven children, and one of them left North Carolina and moved to Brownwood, Comanche County, Texas. His name was John James Allison, and he became a Medical Doctor. Dr. JJ Allison had nine children, one of whom was named William Allison. He was a member of the Texas Rangers Frontier Battalion for a time. William later left Texas with his new wife Julia, and they moved to a small town in Arkansas called Hattieville. He planned to become a farmer. Unfortunately, William left on a wagon to go to the general store one fateful day and he was never heard from him again. The Allison family tree almost ended right there, except that William and his wife Julia had one son before he died. His name was John Washington Allison. His middle name no doubt named after George Washington, our first President. God wanted the Allison family to continue, and so it did.

Hattieville is an area near Morrilton, Arkansas. It is just one little stretch of road on Highway 213. When you first arrive, you see this sign and when you leave, there is another one just like it. I was there recently and the only business that I saw was a store with two old gas pumps outside and a community center. Since Morrilton is only 9.5 miles away, everyone drives there for their needs. The yellow wildflowers were beautiful.

John Washington Allison was a farmer in Hattieville, Arkansas, and he was my great-grandfather. He was married twice. In his first marriage, he had two children, and in his second marriage, he had six more! My grandfather Terry Francis Allison was my great-grandfather's first son from his first marriage. Terry liked people to call him Fred, so everyone knew him as Fred Allison. Fred had four children. Three of those children were girls and one boy: Eva Dean, Betty, Nancy, and my father, Billy Joe Allison. Bill was born in Cabot, Arkansas. Bill Allison had four children. One son by his first marriage, yours truly, with my mother and three other children, two girls, Tami and Kelly, and a boy, Jon, by his second marriage to Margaret, whom he met in Texas towards the end of his Air Force career.

My first shock in life was when my father died when I was only 17 years old and a senior in high school. Instead of looking forward to graduating high school and going to college, I had to deal with my father's death. At the time of his death, he was the Chief of Police at Camden, Arkansas. I will never forget the Arkansas State Police, Camden Police Department, and other law enforcement officers who attended my father's funeral. The law enforcement community knows how to show up for a fallen officer.

Bill had moved to Arkansas to have a relationship with me once I turned eighteen. My parents had divorced soon after I was born. Before that Arkansas law enforcement position, he was the Chief of Police in Grover City (now Grover Beach), California, near where his parents lived in Arroyo Grande, California. Before that, he was a police officer in Arroyo Grande under his brother-in-law, James (Jim) Clark, the Chief of Police in Arroyo Grande. Uncle Jim had married my Aunt Betty. The Arroyo Grande Police Station building is named after my Uncle Jim Clark. He was a legend in that town and a significant influence on my father getting into law enforcement. Here is an old picture of them from their days at the Arroyo Grande police department. My dad is on the right, and my Uncle Jim is on the left. My Uncle Jim was very helpful to me after my father died. I will never forget his kindness to me.

My father was born in 1934 and grew up during World War II. This war had a patriotic effect on him because when he was only 15 years old and with his parent's permission, he joined the Army in February of 1950. Soon after joining, he was shipped out to fight in the Korean War. He told the Army he was 16, and they let him join. Bill Allison became a paratrooper in the 187th E Company. He had two combat jumps into North Korea. One before his 16th birthday, seven months after joining the Army and he made another combat jump soon afterward, in December of 1950, shortly after turning 16 years old. Can you imagine jumping out of a plane like this into North Korea as a 15 or 16-year-old teenager? (And liberals and progressives get offended by tweets!) Sorry about the picture quality, as it is 70 years old, but you can see what I mean. There is not an ounce of fear in my father's facial expression. He was loaded down and ready to jump!

He spent six years and six months in the Army and had an honorable discharge while earning a few medals along the way. Right before he got out of the Army, the 187th merged into the 101st Airborne, and so, he bought a 101st Airborne tattoo to celebrate. He was a member of the "Rakkasans," which is the name given to their unit from the Japanese when they were stationed there after World War II and during the Korean War. Loosely translated, it means falling umbrella or parachute. His unit won a Presidential Unit Citation. He was not a four-star General or anything, but I was proud of his accomplishments. He served a little over ten years and six months for our country in the Army and the Air Force. I verified the medals from his DD-214, these pictures, and other pictures. Once verified, I put it all together in this shadow box. I am not the best craftsman, but I felt my father's guidance in building this shadow box. His spirit helped me discover more and more about his service.

When he was discharged from the Army, he met my mother, and about a year later, I was born. He was concerned as a father that he did not have a good enough job to take care of me. As a result, my father joined the Air Force knowing that as a married Airman, he could provide for his new son and family. Here is a picture of them on their wedding day.

Unfortunately, my maternal grandfather did not like that his 19-year-old and only daughter was married at such a young age. Besides, he was not a fan of my father nor his daughter being a military wife with a kid and traveling away from her support system. She was only 20 years old when she had me as her first son. Sadly, they got a divorce soon after I was born. My mother never became a military wife with her new husband. My maternal grandfather was the domineering type. For some reason, he would not let his daughter be a military spouse.

When I went to college, I was still reeling from my father's death. After my father died, I was like a ship without a rudder. I did not know who I wanted to be or what I wanted to major in until I finally decided to major in Criminal Justice in his honor. I had a bad semester in my third year because I worked at a local restaurant late into the night, and I neglected my studies that semester. My tuition funding dried up as a result. You can read between the lines. I moved out when I was 18 years old and never looked back. I wish things were different and I could have known my father, but I know others have worse situations than mine. He was a true American hero to me. Bill Allison was the kind of guy an American Patriot like you would appreciate.

Sometimes people look at divorcing spouses as a bad thing. With me, however, I see the children and grandchildren that would never have been born if it was not for the divorce of my father and my mother. In my mind, their divorce was a good thing. My father remarried and had three children, and my mother did the same. I can tell you that there are some beautiful people on the Allison side of the family and the Johnson side of the family. There are lots of children and grandchildren from both sides.

Here is an old picture of me with my Allison brother Jon and sisters Tami and Kelly, and their mother, Margaret. Sorry, but I am missing a boatload of Allison children and grandchildren. Jon had one son, Riley. Tami had two daughters, Teri and Alyssa. Kelly has three children, Jace, Devin, and Joe. Jace has four children, and Devin has two children. Sadly, we lost Jon and Tami in their early 50s.

Here is a picture of my Johnson family. My son is missing from this photo as he had to work and could not make it back to Arkansas. Also missing is my brother David who died in a car accident in his early thirties, and the father that I grew up with, Hillman Johnson, died in his 50s of cancer.

My sister Sharri has three boys, Jacob (Jake), Jared, and Jensen. My brother David had one daughter, Natalie, whom we call Little Natalie because my wife's name is Natalie. My brother Gary has two boys, Cameron and Collin.

My first son Reese passed away from Sudden Infant Death Syndrome, but my wife and I are blessed with two beautiful children, Marshall and Rudi. Although it was scary after losing Reese, we dusted ourselves off and decided there was no reason to wait to have another child. Marsh was born about fourteen months after Reese. We were on pins and needles about Marsh being at risk for SIDS, but thankfully, he was not. Marshall is the most amazing son. He was my interpreter for Game of Thrones. Ha! We are incredibly proud of him. Marshall is a Service Manager for a Power Sports business here in Jacksonville, Florida.

After Marsh was born, we were like most young parents who thought we would have "x" number of kids but soon discovered miscarriages. We had three miscarriages in a row! Talk about tough. Ugh! After the three miscarriages, the blessing of Marshall came into complete focus. My wife calls him our miracle baby. We did not know if we would ever have another child. After our third miscarriage, one night, we were watching the movie "Rudy." My wife said right then and there that if we had a boy, then we would name him Rudy. If we had a girl, then we would name her Rudi. Of course, we were blessed with a girl. Marshall and Rudi are great examples of having faith and never giving up no matter what challenges that you face in life. Rudi is currently enrolled in Dental School.

Like I said earlier. Many people would have never been born if my father and mother had not divorced. Their divorce was a good thing in my mind, with many blessings that followed.

When you have children, then your kids come first. Finishing my degree was put on hold until I took care of my children's educational needs. That is why it took me a while to finish my degree. At age 60, I finally earned my Bachelor of Arts in Criminal Justice with a Personal Finance Minor from the University of Arkansas at Little Rock.

Today, they call it UA-Little Rock to distinguish it from UA-Fayetteville, the Razorbacks home. I was President of my fraternity, Sigma Alpha Epsilon (ΣAE). Phi Alpha to any readers who are ΣAE brothers! I suppose at age 60 that I did not have to finish my degree, but I do not like leaving things unfinished. With a combination of online UA-Little Rock courses and attending the University of North Florida in person, I put it all together. I came out with my Bachelor of Arts degree. I did the walk, too. I was not going to miss that for the world. Even though I have what most consider to be a liberal arts degree, trust me, I am not a liberal. Sorry to disappoint. Ha!

Shifting gears, my maternal grandmother was a special lady. Her Catholic parents, Joseph and Mary came over from the Portuguese Island of Madeira, so she was 100% Portuguese. She was all of 4'11" tall. Her name was Bernice. When I was a teenager, she made me cottage cheese and green olives. Even today, I always eat my cottage cheese with green olives. This is a little something that I do to honor and remember her. Unfortunately, she ended up with kidney disease, which caused her death. She was long divorced, and on welfare, so she didn't have much of anything, but that made no difference to me. My granny would do things like fix me breakfast, or wash my hair in the sink, and, of course, make me some cottage cheese and green olives. We would just sit and talk while she puffed on Pall Mall cigarettes. I remember talking to her when Elvis died. She was so upset over that. She was a fan of Elvis Presley, like a lot of people. My maternal grandmother had a significant impact on me. She would attend Catholic mass even though she was in immense pain with her kidney disease. After watching her commitment to Jesus Christ during my teenage years, I decided at age 14 that I wanted to become a Catholic like her. She was an excellent example for Christ to me. I moved in with her during her last year of life. I tried to help her as best as I could.

Shifting gears again, I must laugh when I hear liberals and progressives talk about "white privilege." This young man on the right is my paternal grandfather. He is with his little brother Perry Roosevelt Allison. (Another Allison named after a President.) How is this for "white privilege?" I just love this picture. Notice the clothes and the wood on the house. Are these not the most incredible-looking kids?

I am proud to have had a grandfather with a blue-collar upbringing. He was a farmer when he was young. His father, John Washington Allison, taught him how to be a farmer in Hattiesville, Arkansas. Later, he went to work for Kroger delivering milk. Here he is with his Kroger hat.

He was the kind of guy who did what he had to provide for his family. It is called hard work. It is more rewarding than accepting a government handout and not having any self-esteem.

Hopefully, now, you can understand about the Allison clan and my family's background. Our Allison family was here before our country was founded as the great nation it is today. One of my great-grandfathers fought in the Revolutionary War. Wow! I am proud to be an Allison with such a storied history. Perhaps, it will make sense to you now why I named my book as I did with the "for American Patriots" tag.

My ultimate goal was to write a book to help you design a diversified and or focused portfolio while at the same time teaching you about a multitude of investment choices. In addition, I will teach you about the importance of choosing a fiduciary. Further, I will touch on a very important topic, Elder Care and why Elder Law attorneys are so vital. This book will be a "how-to" that you can refer to time and time again for help. I will dispense a few jabs at liberals and progressives along the way that should make you laugh.

We should look forward to great things in the future while having gratitude and respect for our past ancestors. We would not be here without them. Enjoy the read!

CHAPTER ONE

Portfolio Design

Portfolio Design. Those are the two most important words you will ever read regarding investing. Most investors do not take the time to put together a portfolio. Instead, they simply buy things willy-nilly based on something they saw on the Internet or television. Worse, they picked up a stock tip from a friend. Unless your friend is a multi-billionaire, it is probably a bad idea to take a stock tip from your friend.

Before you end up with a final portfolio, you must first decide whether you will manage your own money or hire a professional money manager to do it for you?

Let's look at these two options. The first one is where you manage your own money. With over thirty years of professional financial services experience, I can tell you that teaching you how to do this in a book is a challenge in and of itself. Nevertheless, I plan to meet that challenge and then some. Stick with me. I will make you a Portfolio Designer before you know it.

Okay. You are going to manage your own money. (Sorry if I snicker a little bit, but most of you are woefully unprepared for what I am going to throw at you.) Where do you start? You are going to need a source for researching investments. Of course, my first question is, what will you be investing in exactly? Stocks, Exchange Trade Funds (ETFs), Exchange Traded Notes (ETNs), Mutual Funds, Government Bonds, Mortgage-Backed Bonds, Corporate Bonds, High Yield Bonds, Municipal Bonds, Bank Loans (Floating Rate), Natural Resources, Managed Futures, Options, Currencies, Cryptocurrencies, Real Estate,

Money Market Funds, Certificates of Deposits, Promissory Notes, or Private Placements? Do you want to invest in specific sectors, specific industries, specific countries, Micro-Cap, Frontier Markets, Emerging Markets, or Developed Markets (International/Global)?

Now that we have narrowed it down to a million different investment options, then you know exactly what to invest in, right? You cannot just pick one or two of those and start building your portfolio. We still must do our research. Our research is the bigger question. Where can you get research on most, if not all, of the above investment options? Good question. A follow-up question would be how good the research offered is? Is it just a simple website like Yahoo® Finance or Google® Finance? Perhaps, you may want to subscribe to a service like Morningstar®, Ned Davis, Argus, CFRA, or others for your research. There is a big difference between the research offered by Yahoo® Finance and Morningstar®. Of course, websites like Yahoo® Finance or Google® Finance are free!

How wonderful! Morningstar® has a subscription service. I know. I know. You already have Netflix, Hulu, Apple TV+, Showtime, HBO Max, Discovery +, Paramount, and others. What's one more going to hurt? Morningstar® is the leader in research. All those different investment options mentioned above are covered by Morningstar®, with perhaps limited coverage on cryptocurrencies simply because of their recent arrival on the investing scene. If you were going to pay for research with the most coverage, I would opt for their subscription service. You can find them at, where else? https://www.morningstar.com.

What if you do not want to add a research subscription-like Morningstar®? The next best option is to use the research provided by large investment firms, such as (in alphabetical order) Charles Schwab, E*TRADE, Fidelity, or TD Ameritrade who is soon to be absorbed by Schwab because of their recent merger. If you already have an investment account at one of these firms, you can get your free research! Of course, they will give away a limited amount of free research by visiting their respective websites. Morningstar® provides some of the research to these firms through licensing agreements. However, you can only receive a complete plethora of research from Morningstar's subscription service. By the way, there is nothing in it for me for saying that.

These large brokerage firms have research from other firms, too, but you may not be aware of them. Research firms like Ned Davis, Argus, CFRA, Credit Suisse, Zack's, Refinitiv, and others are available. Each of these research firms has its unique approach. Some may offer ready-made stock or mutual fund portfolios, while others provide a star ranking or top stocks/funds list. Others may offer more of a macroeconomic and sector view. Regardless, which large firm that you choose to do business with, I am sure that you will have more than enough research to look through. You may already have access to these research firms by looking at your brokerage account's research area.

We are going to have to, as Jen Psaki would say, "circle back" to this portfolio design a little later. Unlike her, I have the answers. Sorry to go off track here, but if you did an "um" count on her press conferences, I think you would hear her mutter the word "um" quite a bit. It is a toss-up on how many times she says, "um," and how many times she says, "circle back." I do not mean to beat her up, though. We all probably say, "um," too much, and "circle back" is like her trademark now. Okay, back to work. You do not have all day.

I will break down researching the most important investments to understand in separate chapters, starting with stocks.

CHAPTER TWO
Stock Portfolios

Investing in stocks is fun! Ask the people who sold out of GameStop, ticker symbol GME when it was at its high point. They will tell you. They could pay off their student loans, buy a new house, or car, and other fun stuff with their profits. I suspect that more people lost money in GameStop than made money, but it offers a valuable lesson in investing in stocks. That lesson is that investing in stocks consists of two significant decisions. The first one is the buy decision, and the second and most important one is the sell decision. You must know your sell decision **when you make your buy decision!** Of course, there are two sell decisions. At what price do you sell if the stock goes down? In other words, how much of a loss are you willing to take before you buy the stock? Is it a 5%, 10%, 15%, or 20% loss that you are ready to take? If you choose one of those, then will you unemotionally sell when it hits one of those loss percentages, or will you hesitate and add "hope" into the mix? I would say to forget the hope. Sell and move on. Look for another stock when it hits your downside sell percentage loss. You can always "circle back" to it later.

Of course, not only do you need to make a sell decision on the downside. You, in turn, need to establish upside sell percentages, too. Do you want to have a disciplined sell on the upside percentage, such as 5%, 10%, 15%, or 20%? Or are you more inclined to just let it ride and look at it on an annual basis? The more disciplined you are with your sell decisions, the better off you will be when it comes to investing. Take the emotion out of it!

Whew! That was tough making those decisions, wasn't it? Never fear. I will help you struggle through it all.

CHAPTER THREE

Sectors and Industries

Let's look at stocks from a Sector and Industry standpoint. There are eleven different sectors. The main ones are Communication Services, Consumer Discretionary, Consumer Staples, Energy, Financials, Health Care, Industrials, Materials, Real Estate, Technology, and Utilities. Within each of these sectors, you can break them further into specific industries.

Okay, now tell me. Which of those sectors are the best ones? There are eleven of those sectors, by the way. Which of those eleven sectors are the right ones to be in today looking out into the future? You cannot know without doing your research. According to S&P Dow Jones Indices, Index Dashboard: US for December 31, 2020, the following sectors performed as follows for the calendar year 2020:

Information Technology	43.89%
Consumer Discretionary	33.30%
Communication Services	23.61%
Materials	20.73%
Health Care	13.45%
Industrials	11.06%
Consumer Staples	10.75%
Utilities	0.48%
Financials	-1.69%
Real Estate	-2.17%
Energy	-33.68%

The above table shows how each sector performed in 2020. Which of those sectors is going to achieve the best returns in 2021? Here is another decision that you must make. You still have not come close to picking a stock yet.

Let's mull over this sector issue for a moment. Do you want to have a focused stock portfolio in one or two specific sectors that you think will do well in 2021? Or would you like to build a more diversified stock portfolio consisting of stocks in each of the eleven sectors listed above?

If you want a focused stock portfolio, you may want to consider how much of your investable assets you are willing to risk. Are you putting 100%, 80%, 60%, 40%, or 20% of your currently available investing dollars to work? Here we go again. I know. I know. I am making this hard, but you need to think about these things for your own good. You must know your percentages before investing in a focused stock portfolio. You can choose a more aggressive percentage approach first, then back it down later if it proves to be too much to stomach.

I have a question. Which is the riskier approach? A focused stock portfolio investing in only one or two sectors, or a more diversified stock approach investing in all eleven sectors? I think you know the answer. If you chose the focused stock portfolio and then, in turn, put 80 — 100% of your investable stock dollars into it, then you are taking a whole lot more risk than putting 80 — 100% in the diversified stock portfolio. Wouldn't you agree? It just might make more sense to have less of your money in a focused stock portfolio and more in a diversified stock portfolio.

Today is your lucky day! Fractional shares of stocks have arrived! In the old days, you could only buy a stock with a full share, as in one share, ten shares, one hundred shares, and so on. However, due to increased competition among brokerage (trading firms), you can now buy fractional shares of stocks without commissions. Yippee! (One of my favorite words that editors hate.) What this means is that you can design a diversified stock portfolio with $10,000 or even lower if you want. Now, I say that with a caveat. Some of these big brokers will only let you buy specific stocks, like those in the S&P 500®, for example. Other brokerage firms will allow it no matter what stock you want to buy. You must do some homework if you're going to build a focused or diversified portfolio of stocks utilizing fractional shares. In other words, you need to read the fine print, especially the part about fractional shares and any buy or sell restrictions. You cannot just go off willy-nilly without understanding the legalese. I will repeat that statement in another way. You need to know the rules of the game, so **read the fine print**. No willy-nilly investing!

Let's get back to designing a stock portfolio. I want to use $100,000 as our pool of money simply because it is easy to understand from an example standpoint. Ratchet it up or down according to your pool of money.

Okay, let's work on the diversified stock portfolio for now. We will "circle back" to the focused stock portfolio later. We know that we have eleven sectors and $100,000 in our example. A simple calculation would be to invest equally in all eleven sectors. Divide our $100,000 by eleven, and we end up with roughly $9,000 per sector. When we do our stock research, we are now looking for stocks in each sector. This style of investing is called equal-weighting. You do not live or die with equal weighting by over-concentration in one stock.

Let's "circle back" for a second and consider the macro or helicopter view. How many stocks overall do we want in our diversified stock portfolio? It probably makes sense to use eleven as a divisible factor. In other words, if we want around 30 stocks, then we probably want three x's 11 or 33 stocks. If we wanted more stocks, then factor that up by 11 (i.e., 44, 55, or 66). To keep it simple, let's assume that you want a 33-stock portfolio across eleven sectors. This means that you buy three stocks per sector. The math is $3,030 x's 3 stocks per sector

= $9,090 total per sector x's 11 = $100,000 total investment. (That is close enough for government work.)

Things are getting a little easier now. We simply find research on 33 stocks and three per sector, making our sector research easier. We do a screen for each sector and the three stocks we want to purchase. Let's think about the Communications Services sector for a moment. There are sub-sectors within the Communications Services sector. I know what you are thinking. "Rick, you are making things hard again." Sorry, it is my job. Within the Communications Services sector, you can break it down further into the sub-sectors of Interactive Media & Services, Entertainment, Media, Diversified Telecommunication Services, and Wireless Telecommunication Services. Unfortunately, that is five sub-sectors, and we can only buy three stocks in the overall Communications Services sector. I hate to break it to you, but you must make another decision besides that one. Do you want to invest in stocks in the Communications Services sector with higher dividends or higher growth prospects? What about fair value? Fair value is a number derived from Benjamin Graham's book, "Security Analysis," written way back in 1934. According to Graham, stocks valued with a fair value calculation of 1.0 are perfectly fair valued. Stocks with a fair value under 1.0 are considered undervalued. Stocks with a fair value over 1.0 are considered over-valued. Suppose you think about my sector performance table and remember that during 2020, the Energy sector was the worst performer. If we look at the current fair value of stocks in the Energy sector, I bet that we will find undervalued stocks. I **researched** and read a recent Morningstar's Large Cap Stock List - February 2021 and saw that Exxon Mobil had a fair value of 0.61. ConocoPhillips had a fair value of 0.65, and Chevron had a fair value of 0.77. The conclusion is that these stocks are undervalued. Warren Buffet is a fan of fair value investing, by the way.

If we "circle back" to the best performing sector from our table above, the Technology sector, then I bet we will find over-priced stocks.

Doing a quick Technology sector screen in the same Morningstar® Large-Cap Stock List from February 2021, we find that Microsoft is fair valued at 0.95, Apple is fair valued at 1.56, and Cisco is fair valued at 0.93. What does this tell us? Microsoft and Cisco are close to fair value, but Apple is over-priced. Should you buy Apple right now? Would you be better off buying Chevron instead? From a fair value calculation, you should make more money by buying Chevron over Apple because the odds are Chevron will make its way back to fair value while Apple is likely to decline back to fair value. It was recently trading at around $145, but will you look at that? It has dipped down to as low as $116 recently. Maybe there is something to this fair value thing. It is called reversion to the mean for you statistics fans. I wish picking stocks were as simple as determining fair value, but unfortunately, it is not. There is more to consider.

President Joseph Biden (PINO or **P**resident **in** **N**ame **O**nly to some people) has on the www.WhiteHouse.gov[1] website one of his **Climate** priorities. It says,

> "President Biden will take swift action to tackle the climate emergency. The Biden Administration will ensure we meet the demands of science while empowering American workers and businesses to lead a clean energy revolution."

By the way, if you do not like me calling Joe Biden a PINO, then you have permission to burn my book. Just like Joseph Goebbels and his Nazi pals would do. That may make you a Nazi, however, if you do so. RINO or PINO. There is not much difference between them.

Climate emergency? Spare me the drama! There is no climate emergency, except that he laid off over 10,000 Keystone pipeline workers with the stroke of a pen. How about that climate emergency? Or, when windmills kill birds? Or, when solar does not work well in North America?

---

1. http://www.WhiteHouse.gov

I certainly did not see anything in that paragraph on Climate that mentioned oil companies, did you? Therefore, can we conclude that a company like Chevron or Exxon Mobil might have some difficulty because of political issues related to the PINO. Excuse me. I meant Mr. Biden and his administration. Never mind the fact that all the wind turbines just froze solid in Texas during a recent storm in February of 2021. The green energy people want you to believe it is the evil oil companies' fault that the wind turbines froze solid. Liberal politicians are good at **making accusations** like calling everyone a domestic terrorist, racist or white supremacist.

How many damn white supremacists do you personally know? For me, the answer is zero. I bet it is the same with you. There is not a white supremacist problem in America. Like the racism chant, the liberals use their accusations to put good people on the defensive so that **they can control you.** Calling us all domestic terrorists is their new thing. I do not know any domestic terrorists, either. If I did, then I would turn them into law enforcement. Liberals and progressives want to put you and me in a defensive posture because that is how they control you. **Never apologize to these people** because that gives them power. Do not even answer their ridiculous accusations or, better yet, fight back with a vengeance in a non-violent way.

I like Senator Ted Cruz from Texas a lot, but he made a mistake when he apologized and flew back to Texas while on vacation with his family. He should have never done that. Instead, he should have stated that he will return to Texas after his family vacation, and he is currently being kept abreast of the situation. That is all he needed to say. Political leaders are so scared of the "optics." They have to realize that liberals and progressives are **ruthless** in this area, and you only give them more power when you back down. **Never back down! NEVER!** Liberals and progressives start with the everyone is guilty mentality. How are those lockdowns working for you? It is the control over you that they are after. Do you get that? If you disagree with me because I believe in the United States Constitution, then as Rush Limbaugh used to say, "You can go pound sand."

My point, of course, is that just because a stock is under-valued does not mean that it is an excellent place to put your money. I'm sorry if you thought fair value would be the end-all to be all. No such luck with me. I will make you think critically about investing, which is sorely missed these days, especially by uneducated liberals and progressives. They just believe everything they hear, lies and all from the mainstream (fake news) media.

Fair value is one thing to look at, but I want you to look at regular, recurring cash flow. Is the company you want to invest in producing steady, recurring cash flow? Not just revenue, mind you, but revenue plus a profit. An excellent example of this would be a company with a subscription model like Netflix®, or Apple®, Inc. I am just using these two companies as an example. I am not making a recommendation. Both firms have many subscribers who pay each month for their services. This means regular, recurring cash flow and a profit! If a company has steady, recurring cash flow and a profit, then it might be a good candidate for your three stocks for one of your eleven sector choices.

I know. I know. What about growth stocks that pay little to no dividends? Since you are buying three stocks per sector, why not make two regular, recurring cash flow companies with a profit and the other a growth company? Eureka! This way, two-thirds of your diversified stock portfolio will be made up of sound companies, and you will be taking more risk on one stock in each of the 11 sectors. Now you're critically thinking! By the way, applying our trusty math skills, we can surmise that approximately 1/3 or $33,333 of our $100,000 diversified stock portfolio will be in growth stocks. The other two-thirds will be invested in companies with regular recurring cash flow and a profit. It depends on whether you choose stocks with high dividends or stocks with low dividends. Higher dividends will make our stocks value stocks, and lower dividend yields will likely make our stocks more growth-oriented. I know. I know. I am generalizing here, but you get my drift.

Let's "circle back" to sector investing. We will invest in 11 sectors at three stocks per sector, with one of the three being a higher risk growth stock and the other two being more stable regular, recurring cash flow companies with a profit. Do not forget the profit part. Now, you have managed to make the research part a whole lot easier. You simply screen for stocks in each sector and pick two stable firms and one growth-oriented firm. After you do your research on each of the 11 sectors and pick your three stocks per sector, you have your diversified stock portfolio. Of course, if you do not want to take many risks, then eliminate the riskier stocks and build your diversified stock portfolio with all regular, recurring cash flow companies with a profit!

You must think about political issues and pandemic issues, too. We already touched on political matters. Now let us discuss pandemic issues. For example, if we get this vaccine rollout completed this year and can knock the virus down, some companies that benefited from the pandemic may lose their stock values after the pandemic subsides. For example, Zoom Video Communications, ticker symbol ZM has benefited from the pandemic. Still, once the pandemic is over or under control, then the odds are that Zoom's stock will decline at least temporarily. Other examples may be food delivery firms publicly traded like Uber Eats, Door Dash, Grub Hub, and Postmates. These companies may do well long term, but you must assume that they would at least temporarily decline once the pandemic subsides. Investors would look at these delivery firms with greater scrutiny to see how much cash they can generate post-pandemic. Let's pray that we do indeed have a post-pandemic. If you do not believe in the power of prayer, then you ought to try it sometime. It will help you through some tough times. Read a chapter from the Bible every day or as often as you can. It will keep you grounded and on the right path.

Critical thinking is involved in picking stocks. You must consider the future and decide about it. Would you invest in leisure and hospitality right now? Probably not if you are a conservative investor, but perhaps so if you are more aggressive. After the pandemic subsides, people will be ready to get back out there, have some fun, stay at hotels, fly on airplanes, and take a cruise. Do you see? While you are doing your research, keep in mind the future! Nobody has a crystal ball, but we can make good, well-thought-out, critical thinking decisions.

Now I wanted to "circle back" to our focused stock portfolio. First, how many stocks should be in a focused stock portfolio. In my mind, you should have no more than twenty and no less than ten. The more stocks you choose, the more research you will need to perform. It does not make a lot of sense for a focused stock portfolio to risk every penny you own on this type of portfolio. Here is another decision. What percentage of your overall investable assets are you going to commit to a focused stock portfolio? I would say twenty percent to a third of your investable assets, depending on your risk level. This next suggestion applies to both the diversified stock portfolio and the focused stock portfolio. Put the riskier stocks from the diversified stock portfolio in a separate account independently. Do the same for the focused stock portfolio. This will allow you to see how your stocks from the diversified stock portfolio perform and how the focused stock portfolio performs. If you jumble them together, it is much harder to figure out how your riskier or focused stocks are performing.

If you were to look at a mountain chart from 1930 until today that shows asset class performance, then what you will find is small-cap stocks out-performed all other asset classes. There are periods where large-cap or mid-cap stocks outperform small-caps, but over the long haul, small-caps perform the best. If you were trying to build a focused stock portfolio, then you probably want to focus your research on these areas: small-cap, micro-cap, and frontier stocks. There is a lot of risk in this area, but the reward can be, well, rewarding, for lack of a better word. You should stick with small-cap growth stocks primarily and add micro-cap and frontier stocks if you want to add more aggressive risk to your focused stock portfolio. If your focused stock portfolio consists of all small-cap growth, that is perfectly fine. Micro-cap stocks and frontier stocks have a ton of risk, and research is tough to come by in these areas. Getting good execution in micro-cap and frontier stocks can be a challenge, too. However, the more risk you take, the more reward you can potentially earn, but you must be smart about it. Stay away from stocks trading under $5 per share and pink sheet stocks. Those are places where your money goes to die.

A word about investing risk: Small-cap, micro-cap, and frontier companies may be more vulnerable to adverse market conditions, and their securities may be less liquid and experience greater volatility than larger domestic and international companies. Trading these stocks in a fast-moving market can also have adverse consequences. The bid and ask spreads will widen in a fast-moving market, and you must be extremely careful on those types of trading days. You are highly likely to get poor execution of your order, especially for market orders. You need always to remember that there is a middleman between a buyer and a seller of stocks. The middleman's job is to keep the bid and ask spreads manageable and to make a profit! You may put in a market order to sell when the bid is at $10.90 a share but find it executed at $10.25 a share. Generally, this means that the middleman had so many sell orders that he had to keep knocking the price down. I would not lose a ton of sleep over it but selling on days of high volatility is generally not a good idea (**ever**) unless your stock is in a free-fall.

Further, you may think you are okay with limit orders, but you would be mistaken. Stop Limit orders execute at the next price after it hits your limit. Nothing stops a gap down of a small-cap stock in a fast-moving market. Again, you could put in a stop-limit order to sell at $10.90, and the subsequent price is $10.25. Why? Because there are so many orders that the middleman will move the bid price down to compensate. The middleman is not going to take a loss. **They never take a loss**. You do! That is another reason to be calm and remove the emotion from stock investing. Refrain from trading on volatile days!

You can find some free looks at small-cap stocks, micro-cap stocks, or frontier stocks by simply going to an Exchange Traded Fund company website, finding their ETFs that invest in those types of funds, then look inside at what they are holding. Pick from that list to do your research. Otherwise, you could just buy their small-cap, micro-cap, or frontier ETF and quit wasting your time researching stocks and enjoy your life.

Now you know how to invest in stocks.

CHAPTER FOUR

Portfolio Design Issues

Before you build your diversified or focused ETF or mutual fund portfolio, it is essential to understand what duplicity may be lurking in your choices of asset classes. Duplicity is another term for stock overlap. In my own opinion, too much stock overlap can ruin a diversified portfolio.

The first thing that you must understand when you are a designer of diversified or focused portfolios is that every decision you make is not correct. You want to have most of your decisions be good ones. You cannot build a diversified or focused portfolio and have every asset class that you choose be correct for every given period. You will have some hits and misses because of correlation. I will explain more about correlations a little bit later.

My advice is not to be afraid to cut and run or find something better. Do not second guess your sell decisions. Take the emotions out of it. If your asset class is on a ski slope downhill, then sell it and invest in another asset class.

Now I want to "circle back" to when I was talking about poor portfolio design decisions made by others or stock overlap. I cannot tell you how many times I evaluate portfolios by big institutional money management firms who make duplicity mistakes. I like to compare how I am doing for my clients to them. If I am beating them during 1, 3, 5, or 10-year periods, then I know that I am on the right track. These institutional money managers typically will buy a large-cap value fund and a large-cap growth fund. What is wrong with this? They have just made themselves a large-cap blend or core fund. They could have just bought one large-cap blend or core fund and accomplished the same thing. (Blend = core, by the way.) Another mistake that I see is they will have multiple large-cap growth funds. They may have two or three large-cap growth funds. By the way, your local insurance agent who has a securities license does this all the time. (Hopefully, you have not invested your money with your local insurance agent!) These institutional money managers may buy a large-cap index fund and then buy two actively managed large-cap growth funds. All three of these funds' top holdings will be eerily similar. Why? Well, the large-cap index fund will be buying the index. The other two will not deviate too far from the index or risk underperforming the index. They will try to "actively" manage their fund and add alpha which in layman's terms means to earn a return more than you can make with the index.

It is kind of like taking 1/3 of your overall portfolio and focusing it on riskier stocks, or Core and **Explore,** as discussed earlier. The problem with this three-fund strategy is you are essentially buying three index funds. This duplicity complicates things, and the bang for the buck will not be there. It is challenging to add alpha (excess return) in the large-cap growth area over and above the index. Actively managed funds always have higher expenses because you are essentially paying for their expertise. However, if they are not exceeding the large-cap index's return, why pay more money in expenses? That's a good question.

Actively managed funds have their place, but if you look closely at the large-cap growth asset class, then you will discover that this <u>is not</u> where to put actively managed money. The actual alpha from investing in actively managed funds is found in micro-cap companies, smaller companies, frontier markets, emerging markets, and international or global markets <u>where good research is harder to come by</u>. Think about large-cap firms like Apple, Amazon, Alphabet, IBM, Bank of America, Tesla, and others. If there is any news on those companies, it is disseminated instantly on the news wires. There is limited news information with less followed stocks and those stocks in foreign countries. There are investment firms (mutual funds and ETFs) with people who live in these areas and know the culture, the trends, the people, and the businesses. The odds are that you and I do not know anything about investing in Singapore or South Korea, but specific ETF and mutual fund companies do. If you favor actively managed asset classes and are looking to add alpha (excess return over the index), focus your attention on the micro-cap companies, smaller companies, frontier markets, emerging markets, international or global markets. Otherwise, just buy the index in these areas if you want to keep it simple.

Another area of portfolio design that I often see is too much exposure in any particular asset class. Suppose you have chosen your 12 — 20 different asset classes. However, if you put 50% in large-cap stocks, your portfolio will live and die based on what the large-cap stock asset class does, and you will not have a diversified portfolio. It would meet the definition of a focused portfolio. This could be fine and dandy if your goal were to have a portfolio focused on large-cap stocks. For a diversified portfolio, this would be, as President Trump liked to say, "a disaster."

In a diversified portfolio, you should set upper limits and lower limits. Generally, you would put an upper limit of 15% if you have around 12 asset classes. If you wanted to spread things out into 20 asset classes, you might wish to a 7.5% — 10% upper limit. By lower limit, I mean the minimum percentage to put into an asset class. For example, if you invest in a particular asset class, you want to invest at least 5% in it.

Further, you may look at the cash or cash equivalents asset class as low as 2.5%. After all, your emergency cash should not be in your investing account, therefore having as little as 2.5% is perfectly acceptable unless you are investing money to pay down your mortgage in an investment account, as I discussed earlier. Even then, I would open a separate brokerage account for those savings and keep the cash allocation between 2.5 — 5%. If you look at my table again, you can see those upper and lower limits.

Asset Classes	Percentage to Invest	Upper Limit Percentage	Lower Limit Percentage
Large-cap		20%	5%
Mid-cap		10%	5%
Small-cap		10%	5%
Developed Markets		15%	5%
Emerging Markets Stocks		10%	5%
Ultra-Short-term Bonds		5%	2.5%
Short-term Bonds		10%	5%
Intermediate-term Bonds		10%	5%
Long-term Bonds		10%	5%
International Bonds		10%	5%
Emerging Markets		10%	5%
Sovereign Bonds		10%	5%
Alternatives/ Sectors		20%	5%
Cryptocurrencies		10%	5%
Cash and equivalents		10%	2.5%

This table is just an example template. You can build your own. Once you understand your upper and lower limits, then you make your choices in each asset class within those limits. If you tend to be more aggressive, you will weight your asset class choices more towards the stocks asset classes and include more in alternatives or specific sectors and perhaps cryptocurrencies. If you were middle-of-the-road or a moderate investor, then you would split your dollars across all the asset classes within those upper and lower limits. If you are more conservative, then you simply reduce your stock asset classes down to the lower limits and increase your bonds asset classes towards the upper limits. However, you always must look to the future with bonds. Are we in a declining interest-rate environment, or are we in an increasing interest rate environment? If you know the answer to that question, you know whether you can weight your bond asset classes towards short and intermediate-term bonds or long-term bonds. It is a sound strategy to always have money towards the upper limit on emerging markets and international bonds. Go short or long-term based on the current interest rate environment.

Correlation is another term to be familiar with, and I touched on this a little bit by discussing stock overlap and duplicity. When you design your portfolio, you want it diversified and diversified by its very nature means putting asset classes together that do not all correlate together. Large-cap, mid-cap and small-cap are going to be correlated together. This is okay if you have other asset classes that are not correlated with those equity asset classes, like ultra-short-term, short-term, intermediate-term, long-term, emerging markets, and international bonds. Real estate, natural resources, and precious metals would be other asset classes that do not correlate so much with stock asset classes.

Other asset classes that you may want to consider are **Factors**. There are numerous Factors like buyback, high beta, momentum, quality, growth, equal-weighting, high dividend, pure growth, pure value, revenue-weighted, low volatility, and minimum volatility. There are plenty of ETFs and mutual funds based on **Factors**. You can kind of go wild these days on splitting asset classes. For example, you could take your large-cap asset class and break it down by utilizing momentum, high beta, equal-weighting, and low volatility and spreading your large-cap asset class dollars across those four. However, you are back to the stock overlap issue again when you do that. It would be tough to avoid any stock overlap, especially if you are spreading out your asset class dollars, but you can certainly minimize the stock overlap. Here is another decision to make. Do you keep things simple, or do you try and add your alpha? Keeping things simple would be to invest in a large-cap blend or core fund and no other large-cap funds. After all, you can never do worse than the index. When you try and add aggressive alpha, you may want to slant your large-cap dollars towards high beta and momentum. If you are more moderate, choosing all four of those Factor asset classes mentioned above may work for you. If you are the conservative type, then slanting your large-cap dollars towards equal-weighting and low or minimum volatility would be your choice. You do the same kind of critical thinking for your asset classes with these choices. I can tell you that large-cap, mid-cap, small-cap, developed markets, and emerging markets have **Factor** categories you can choose from in your portfolio design. When you think about why I said 12 — 20 different investments to build your diversified portfolio, you will realize how easy it is to reach the 20 different investments instead of the more simplified 12 investments. In the end, the choice is all yours.

CHAPTER FIVE

ETFs

Exchange-Traded Funds or ETFs are essentially mutual funds that trade like a stock. Some of the ETF firms with a large selection of fund choices are Avantis, DFA, Fidelity, First Trust, Global X, Invesco, iShares, JP Morgan, PIMCO, ProShares, Schwab, SPDR, VanEck, Vanguard, WisdomTree, and Xtrackers. Of course, there is a multitude of over 2,500 ETF funds available, with more and more added each year. Look for ETFs that have been around for at least three years. It makes for good research.

When you think about building your diversified stock portfolio, you are essentially creating your own ETF. Some people enjoy buying stocks, plus have the time and expertise to do it. In comparison, other people who are too busy or who work for a living would instead leave things up to the professionals. This is where ETFs come in. Nevertheless, if you want to build a diversified ETF or focused ETF portfolio, then you have come to the right place. Even if you leave it to the professionals, then with this book, you will have a working knowledge of how professionals build ETF portfolios. That is the professionals who know what they are doing.

The significant advantage of ETFs is in their creation and redemption. Big institutional investors buy ETFs and sell them. The ETF firm can hand a basket of stocks to the big institution instead of liquidating positions and causing a tax issue to the remaining shareholders of the ETF. Let me explain. Suppose a big institution bought a million dollars of an ETF of the S&P 500® index. When the big institution wants to sell their ETF position, the ETF firm hands them all the stocks in the S&P 500® calculated based on that day's prices. This makes an ETF very tax-efficient for its shareholders. This is not true with mutual funds. You get left holding the tax bag when other shareholders bail. I will "circle back" to mutual fund taxation in another chapter. Now that we got that out of the way, we can move on to building a diversified ETF portfolio and other ETF portfolio strategies.

Let's start with a diversified ETF portfolio. There is a standard method of doing this that won a Nobel Prize, albeit decades ago now. It is called Modern Portfolio Theory. This theory was based on mutual funds, correlation, and asset classes. By the way, you Rush Limbaugh fans will know the difference between a theory and a theorem. A theory is presented as accurate, while a theorem is true. Since ETFs have the same type of correlations and asset classes as explained in the Modern Portfolio Theory thesis paper, it works even better because of the tax advantages described above. The thinking with Modern Portfolio Theory is that certain investments correlate differently from others.

An easy example of this is stocks and bonds. Stocks are more volatile than bonds. Therefore, it stands to reason that they do not correlate together. However, large-cap stocks, mid-cap, and small-cap stocks would closely correlate. Consequently, you would not have as much of a diversified portfolio if all you did was own large-cap, mid-cap, and small-cap stocks. You would want to add things like corporate bonds, emerging market stocks and bonds, foreign bonds, micro-cap stocks, precious metals funds, real estate funds, Treasury bonds, and mortgage-backed securities. These are all considered asset classes. There are more asset classes to choose from than those mentioned above, but those are some of the main ones. You start with the macro view of looking at ETFs in specific asset classes. Then you choose those that do not necessarily correlate with the rest. Do not worry. I will "circle back" and clear things up.

There are different ways to put together a diversified ETF portfolio. One way is to simply pick 12 — 20 distinct asset classes that do not correlate precisely alike, and wallah, you have built your diversified ETF portfolio. Another way is to create what is known as a **Core and Explore** approach. This means that you choose the major asset classes like large-cap, mid-cap, small-cap, short-term bonds, intermediate bonds, long-term bonds, real estate, emerging market stocks, and bonds, then you overlay specific bets or the Explore portion on top. What specific bets? Things like precious metals, micro-cap, frontier stocks, or sectors like technology or health care. Assuming we have the same $100,000 to invest, with a Core and Explore approach, sometimes called a Core and Satellite approach, then you would invest about $75,000 — $80,000 in the Core portion and the balance into the Explore portion. With 75 — 80%, you are taking a diversified approach. With the Explore portion, you are being riskier with about 20 — 25% of your overall investable assets.

I hate to complicate things, but what the heck. It is my nature. Within the Core asset classes, there could be a multitude of choices. For example, the large-cap asset class may include large-cap value, blend or core, and growth, too. Further, it may consist of equal-weighting, fundamental weighting, or market-weighting. Let me explain each. Value ETFs are ETFs that hold companies that have fallen out of favor. If you recall my fair value explanation, you will know that under-valued means underpriced. In the last ten years, the value category has done poorly, in my opinion. Will it do better in the next ten years? Nobody knows for sure, but perhaps you may want to allocate some of your dollars in value stocks if you think in a contrarian manner.

The blend or core asset class category is essentially the index, like the S&P 500® index, the S&P 400® index, or the S&P 600® index. It depends on what asset class you are looking at, but there is an index for just about all asset classes. Here is what to know about investing in blend or core asset classes. If you invest in a blend or core fund, you will get a return that closely resembles the index, minus management expenses. Therefore, you can safely assume that you will never do worse than the index when investing in the blend or core ETFs. By the way, this is what you want. This is a crucial point to understand when evaluating your investments. I will "circle back" to this later, but this is your question when assessing performance. "Is it the asset class that is performing poorly, or the ETF?"

Of course, the growth category is a bet on large-cap, mid-cap, or small-cap growth stocks. Most of these ETFs based on growth are market-weighted, which means they tend to own the high-flyers in their asset class. For example, in the large-cap area, a large-cap growth ETF would likely have Apple, Amazon, Facebook, Netflix, and Alphabet (Google) as their top holdings. Different index providers may have slight differences in their index composition, but most index providers will have a similar makeup, except perhaps in different percentages. An example would be S&P 500® versus the Russell 1000®. Both would have the same stocks mentioned above, but the difference would be that the S&P 500® has 500 stocks in it and the Russell 1000® has 1,000 stocks in it. Which one is more diversified? That's easy, the Russell 1000® because it holds 1,000 stocks instead of 500, thus, it is more diversified. By the way, the Russell 2000® is the next 2,000 stocks after the first 1,000 stocks. The Russell 3000® is the combination of the Russell 1000® and the Russell 2000®. I just wanted to explain that in case you were wondering.

Do you want a more focused ETF portfolio? If so, then perhaps an ETF based on the S&P 500® might offer a little better return over the long haul since it is more concentrated. If you are more conservative, then you may prefer an ETF based on the Russell 1000® in your portfolio for your large-cap asset class portion. You can do the same in the mid-cap and small-cap areas by investing in the Russell 2000®, or the S&P 400® plus the S&P 600®. Again, the combination of the S&P 400® and the S&P 600® totals 1,000 stocks while the Russell 2000® is 2,000 stocks. By the way, the S&P 1500® is the S&P 500®, S&P 400® and the S&P 600® added together. If you are a more conservative investor, you might want to go with the Russell index. If you want a more focused approach, then perhaps, the S&P indexes are the way to go. You can choose value, blend (core), or growth in each of these asset classes, too.

Fundamental or equal-weighting are two other areas you can choose within the large-cap, mid-cap, or small-cap asset classes. First, I want to explain the differences between equal-weighting, fundamental and market-weighting. Equal-weighting means that if you were to look at an S&P 500® equal-weighted ETF, you would see that all 500 stocks hold similar percentages (i.e., 2%). In this case, since there are 500 stocks, then each stock would represent an equal percentage (2%) as all the other stocks in an equal-weighting ETF.

Fundamental analysis is a construction method using gross revenue, equity book value, gross sales, gross dividend, cash flow, and total employment as weights. It is a process championed by Research Affiliates®. There is a lot of explaining to understand how fundamental indexes are constructed, so I will not go into that here. It is kind of like looking at the sausage being made. You do not want to know. Your eyes will glaze over, and you will become very confused. You should understand that fundamental indexes have a well-thought-out and researched strategy behind them. Further, I am only providing the Research Affiliates® web site address here if you want to learn more about fundamental analysis. https://www.researchaffiliates.com/en_us/home.html.

Market-weighting is where the weighting percentages are based strictly on the index itself, like S&P 500®. So, whatever S&P indexes say should be in Apple, Amazon, or other stocks, then that is the percentage it should hold. You may see 5 or 6% in the top five holdings, and therefore, your S&P 500® ETF will be market-weighted to the top five holdings. A stock contributing 0.30% to the overall ETF will not have as much effect as a stock that is a 6% holding in a market-weighted index.

Now that you understand the difference between equal-weighting, fundamental analysis, and market-weighting, then you should be able to surmise which ones are more aggressive and which ones are more conservative. It's obvious! The equal-weighted ETF is more conservative than the market-weighted because it does not take as much risk, whereas the market-weighted ETF is concentrated in a handful of top holdings. The ETFs based on fundamental analysis is more conservative than market-weighted ETFs because they focus on undervalued companies. It is anyone's guess whether equal-weighted or fundamental analysis ETFs are more or less conservative than the other. They out-perform each other at different periods, so do not lose any sleep over it.

Here you go with another decision. Do you want to build your diversified ETF portfolio while making a bet on value or growth, or would you be just as happy with the blend or core choice for your asset class? Remember, you cannot do worse than the index with the blend category.

You may be wondering about drilling down even further and choosing equal-weighting, fundamental analysis, or market-weighting. It depends on how aggressive you want to be. Market-weighting is going to be more aggressive than equal-weighting or fundamental analysis.

Now let's move on to which asset classes should be in your Core portion. You should consider large-cap, mid-cap, small-cap, developed markets (global or international), and emerging markets on the equity side, which would make up your Core asset classes.

For the fixed income side, this is a little trickier. It depends on whether we are in a declining interest rate environment or a rising interest rate environment. However, the percentages would change in those types of interest rate environments. The actual Core fixed income choices would be ultra-short-term, short-term, intermediate-term, long-term, high yield, emerging markets bonds, international bonds, and sovereign debt. Ultra-short-term is generally less than three years. You may be asking what is short-term then? Short-term is less than five years, intermediate-term is typically 5 — 10 years, and long-term is more than ten years.

The most conservative fixed-income choice is short-term treasuries. A little more aggressive choice is short-term corporate bonds. So, that is your choice in the three main fixed income categories: short-term treasuries or short-term corporates, intermediate-term treasuries, or intermediate-term corporates, or long-term treasuries or long-term corporates. I would only add ultra-short-term if you are conservative. Plus, I would add corporate high yield if you want to increase your dividend yield on your overall fixed income portion of your diversified portfolio.

The international bond category is simply corporations domiciled overseas. The sovereign debt category is debt (bonds) issued by governments of foreign countries. Riskier sovereign debt like emerging market bonds typically come in two flavors. One asset class flavor is emerging market bonds denominated in US dollars. The other flavor is those denominated in the issuing country's local currency. The safer alternative is always the one denominated in US dollars, but the local currency flavor may be more appealing in certain situations. You are not going to make a big mistake either way because you will not be risking too much of your investable assets in either one of these two flavors of asset classes.

Let's recap. We have large-cap, mid-cap, small-cap, developed markets, emerging markets on the equity side. We have ultra-short-term, short-term, intermediate-term, long-term, high yield, emerging market bonds, developed (international) market bonds, sovereign debt bonds, and cash or cash equivalents. Our investment table would look like this:

Large-Cap Stocks	0%
Mid-Cap Stocks	0%
Small-Cap Stocks	0%
Developed Markets Stocks	0%
Emerging Markets Stocks	0%
Ultra-Short-term	0%
Short-term Bonds	0%
Intermediate-term Bonds	0%
Long-term Bonds	0%
High Yield Bonds	0%
Sovereign Debt Bonds	0%
International Bonds	0%
Emerging Market Bonds	0%
Cash or Cash Equivalents	0%

You probably noticed that there is a 0% for each asset class. That is because we are not ready to put in a percentage just yet. We still have some decisions to make. As far as your investable assets are concerned, are you counting your emergency fund? Hopefully, you are not doing that. Keep the emergency funds separate from investable assets.

Looking at things from a helicopter view or macro view, we need to decide what our equity percentage is going to be for our overall ETF portfolio. Is it going to be 100%, 80%, 60%, 40%, 20% or 0%? What percentages are going to have the most volatility? If you are an engineer, then you likely spent countless hours coming up with 72.3987% as your percentage. Just kidding! The ETF portfolio between 85% and 100% stocks will be the most volatile. I do not want to get too much into the weeds here, but investing 85 or 90% in equities (stocks) is going to add a tiny bang for your buck compared to a more diversified portfolio of 65 to 70% equities. Why? Because of the larger swings in volatility.

I will dumb this down, but it should be easier to understand. The long-term return rate for a 90% ETF stocks portfolio will return, for example, about 13%. The standard deviation of two times 13% means that the range of returns for a 90% ETF stocks portfolio is 26% on the upside and negative (-)26% on the downside. However, this is not entirely accurate, but it is suitable for example purposes. I will "circle back" to this in a moment.

A 65% ETF stock portfolio has an expected return of roughly 8.45% over the long term. At first glance, you would rather make the 13% as opposed to 8.45%, but I have some bad news for you. Markets do not move in a straight line, so you must take the ups and the downs. Two standard deviations of 8.45% mean that your upside range is 16.90%, and your downside risk is negative (-)16,90%. Again, this is for example purposes.

How can a 65% ETF stocks portfolio beat a 90% ETF stocks portfolio? As a result of taking on less risk and volatility. Here is your proof. Let's assume you invest $100,000 in a 90% ETF stocks portfolio and another $100,000 in a 65% ETF stocks portfolio. Immediately after investing, the market goes down a lot at the end of the first year. Your 90% portfolio is down 26%, and your 65% portfolio is only 16.9%. The 65% portfolio beat the 90% portfolio by 9.1%. Now, I want you to put on your critical thinking hat. By losing 26%, your 90% portfolio of $100,000 is now only worth $74,000. Contrast with your 65% portfolio worth $83,100 after losing 16.9%. What does it take in return for each to make it back to breakeven? It takes 35.14% for the 90% stocks portfolio and 20.34% for the 65% stocks portfolio. Now that you understand this fact, you can also understand that a 90% stocks portfolio is like the Hare, and the 65% stocks portfolio is like the Tortoise.

The only way the Hare can stay ahead of the Tortoise is if the time horizon is long, long, and longer. Human nature, as is it, let me ask you, how would you feel about losing $26,000 of your $100,000 portfolio after just one year? I'll tell you what most people do. They get emotional and assume that their ETFs' choices were horrible and sell out. What happened **was supposed to occur** with a 90% stocks portfolio. Does that make sense? In other words, a 90% stocks portfolio is going to do what a 90% stocks portfolio is going to do. In the same vein, the 65% stocks portfolio will do what a 65% stocks portfolio will do. You just must decide where you want your portfolio to be along the risk spectrum and, more importantly, if you can stomach the volatility. Factor in that time horizon because it makes a difference. Your time horizon will tell you if you can be more aggressive or not.

Once you know how much risk and volatility you can take, you simply fill in the fixed income portion, but how do you do that? Do not worry, my friend. I am here to help you.

You have another one of those choices to make. Let's look at the US fixed income market first. We will look at foreign fixed income in a bit. Do you go with the most conservative fixed-income government bonds choice, or do you choose the higher-yielding corporate bonds from the US? We have treasury bills, treasury notes, and treasury bonds in the government category. (More on government bonds in a later chapter.) You can buy ETFs that purchase these bonds in different maturities, such as an ETF with bonds maturing in specific years, like 2024, 2025, 2026, etc. These are commonly used to make a bond ladder. A process where when a bond matures, you replace it with a bond of the longest maturity. In other words, if you have a 7-year bond ladder when the one-year matures, then you buy a 7-year maturity bond because the two-year bond is now a one-year bond after the first year has elapsed. Your formerly three-year bond is now a two-year bond. Your four-year bond is now a three-year and so on. Do you see? If not, reread this paragraph, and it will make sense. This bond ladder strategy is a conservative way of investing in bond ETF's.

Government bond ETFs are packaged in the following macro-categories: ultra-short-term, short-term, intermediate-term, long-term governments, and treasury inflation protection bonds. Let me "circle back" to yields on government bond ETFs. The yields are paltry, but if safety is what you are after, then US government bills, notes, bonds, and inflation-protected bonds are the safest choice if you buy them directly. There is a crazy amount of work to buy them directly, and the big institutions snap up the inventory. Your best bet is going to be to buy US government ETFs. However, in most cases, when you buy US government ETFs, there is nothing guaranteed about them, but it is the next best thing to buying them directly from the US government.

If you decided on US government ETFs, you now must decide how to split your fixed-income dollars amongst them. The first question you want to ask yourself is, "Where are we on the interest rate yield curve?" Have interest rates been on the decline lately, or have they been increasing? What is the future of interest rates? This investing stuff is getting complicated, isn't it? If rates have already declined and are likely to go back up, then you want to stay in the ultra-short-term, short-term, and perhaps short-term inflation-protected government categories. Conversely, if rates are high and declining, then the best place is intermediate-term and long-term. This advice goes for the US government as well as corporate bond ETFs.

Of course, as with everything in life, you have choices. You can choose to go with all US government bond ETFs, or corporate bond ETFs, or a combination of both. Don't forget that we have not discussed international and foreign bond ETFs yet. Go with US government bond ETFs if you are a scaredy-cat and want to be safe, but I am here to tell you that you might as well stick those dollars in a coffee can and bury it in the back yard. You will not be happy with the performance, especially in the ultra-short-term, short-term, and even intermediate-term categories. You will only be satisfied with long-term bonds when interest rates are declining. You will hate long-term when rates rise because you will lose, lose, and lose some more.

I have rambled on long enough about US government ETFs. Let's discuss corporate bond ETFs. We have an extra category called high yield ETFs that we do not have with US government ETFs. You can also find ultra-short-term, short-term, intermediate-term, and long-term high yield ETFs within the high yield ETF category. If there is such a thing in the high yield ETF arena, the safest is to stay ultra-short-term or short-term. You will get a decent yield over regular corporate bonds and keep your maturity short, which will reduce your portfolio risk.

I think you can see where I am going with corporate bond ETFs. You can spread your fixed-income dollars across five different fixed-income asset classes. Again, you must decide where interest rates are heading. If they are increasing, then you want to stay with shorter maturities. If they are declining, you can go with the intermediate and longer maturities ETFs.

You may have noticed that I did not mention anything about preferred stocks ETFs that pay very high dividends. They are in the fixed income category because of how they are built. Some corporations issue them with 50-year maturities. Okay, my exemplary student. What happens to long maturity investments when interest rates go up? They get crushed. Preferred stocks ETFs get crushed, too. I would stay far away from them for this reason. Also, they can suspend their dividends, and you are last on the list in case of a corporation with cash flow issues. Preferred stock dividends are the first thing that gets suspended. Guess what else? You still must pay taxes on the preferred stock dividend you are not getting. Huh? Yes, that is a true statement. Do not blame me. I am not the IRS. The point is that I would not want any preferred stocks ETFs anywhere near my diversified or focused stock portfolio if I were you. Once again, I saved you millions of dollars by telling you about preferred stocks and preferred stocks ETFs.

The other major categories of fixed income ETFs are sovereign bonds, global and international (developed markets), and emerging market bonds. Typically, on these ETFs, you let the ETF itself choose how to spread the money among ultra-short-term, short-term, intermediate-term, or long-term. You let these managers select the companies or countries' quality, too. Yes, you are off the hook in that you do not have to figure out what is going on in Singapore, Hong Kong, or with a company like Tencent. It is hard enough to keep up with the US government or corporations, much less some companies in a foreign country.

You can get exotic in ETFs' fixed income category if you want to, but this is where you get into trouble. Asset classes like bank-loan, local currencies, and other categories. You are opening a can of worms when you start adding these fixed income asset classes, and the risk goes way up. Have you ever seen a bank-loan fixed income product blow up? I have. It is not pretty.

Have you ever seen a preferred stock go from $25 per share down to $19 per share? I have. That is a 24% loss, by the way, and it often happens with preferred stocks while you were sleeping before you can do anything about it. Do not forget it will take a 31.58% return to get that preferred stock price back to $25 per share. Stay away from preferred stocks or preferred stocks ETFs. They are bad for you.

Do you understand currencies, especially in emerging markets like Turkey or Saudi Arabia? If not, it is probably a good idea to stay far away from local currency funds. You have plenty to choose from for your fixed income. You do not need these exotics that complicate things.

The astute reader may have also noticed that I did not include mortgage-backed securities. The reason is that they are subject to refinancing. A certain portion of mortgage-backed securities is refinanced every year. This means that their fund's returns are negatively impacted for the mortgage-backed ETF. Sometimes they will take a big hit on your principal. I do not like them because I feel they have no place in a diversified ETF portfolio. I am not afraid to take a stand, even if mortgage-backed fund managers do not like it. Good people do not apologize for taking a stand. Now, let's build the fixed income portion.

Ultra-Short-term Bonds	0%
Short-term Bonds	0%
Intermediate-term Bonds	0%
Long-term Bonds	0%
High Yield Bonds	0%
Sovereign Debt (Bonds)	0%
International Bonds	0%
Emerging Markets Bonds	0%

The percentages are up to your level of risk. Lean towards ultra-short, short-term, intermediate-term ETFs if you are more conservative. Lean the other way if you are more aggressive with long-term, high yield, sovereign, international, and emerging market bond ETFs. Middle-of-the-road are you? Then, spread your fixed-income dollars across all these categories. Do not forget about factoring in the direction of interest rates. You may need to go short-term and more conservative today, then change later after rates have settled in at a new interest rate high.

You have a track to run on to build an ETF portfolio that includes both stock ETFs, fixed income ETFs, and cash. I did not forget the cash portion. I would keep 2.5 — 10% in cash. This is not where you keep emergency fund money! This is cash as the asset class part of your overall ETF portfolio diversification. There is no need to put much more than 10% in cash since interest rates on money markets, and bank sweep funds are pretty much non-existent these days. All you are doing with your cash portion is reducing the portfolio's overall risk. Well, there you have it. You are all set on building your ETF portfolio.

CHAPTER SIX

ETNs

Exchange-Traded **Notes** or ETNs are different from Exchange-Traded Funds or ETFs. ETNs are subject to the issuer's creditworthiness. It is an **unsecured** debt security issued by a bank. For you folks in Rio Linda, that means high risk. A lot of the leveraged and inverse funds are ETNs. They bet on an index's direction up or down, and they pay based on that, too. In other words, they can be profitable, or they can lose money.

The most important thing to understand about ETNs is by comparing an S&P 500® ETN to an S&P 500® ETF. The S&P 500® ETF holds the stocks of the S&P® 500. The ETN does not contain any stocks. Come again? It holds futures and options based on the S&P 500®. That is a big difference. Wouldn't you rather own the stocks instead of a portfolio of unsecured futures and options? That's what I thought.

With an ETN, if the futures and options bets are incorrect, you can lose boo-coo amounts of money. Stick with ETFs instead. You will be better off buying ETFs for your diversified or focused portfolio. ETN issuers try and trick you. They have ticker symbols just like ETFs. Therefore, you need to make sure that you are not buying an ETN when you wanted to buy an ETF. Double-check your work! You will be glad that you did.

CHAPTER SEVEN

Mutual Funds

Mutual funds versus ETFs. From an asset class perspective, they are pretty much the same. There are a few differences that you need to know. Sometimes, you can find very specialized mutual fund managers who are very good at beating their respective benchmark or index. Most of the time, you will find this in the international arena, but occasionally, you can see this in the US stock market, too. From a fixed income perspective, there are not many fixed income managers who outperform their category benchmark consistently for two reasons. One reason is that there is generally limited inventory for them to buy, and the second reason is there is not as much of an opportunity to outperform on the fixed income side without taking a lot of risk. Usually, you will find a fixed income mutual fund that occasionally outperforms for a year or so, but when things turn south (interest rates change), it is hard to sell at a reasonable price in the fixed income market. In other words, they cannot get out fast enough to avoid losses. Therefore, you will see losses in the fixed income area that pretty much wipes out any prior year gains. Instead of outperformance in the mutual fund fixed income area, you are better off utilizing the asset class selection process mentioned under the Exchange-Traded Funds chapter. Your out-performance will be found in stocks or stock ETFs and mutual funds.

One thing you must be aware of concerning mutual funds is the taxation aspect. If you have ever owned a mutual fund, you know what I am discussing here, but I want to explain it differently. With mutual funds, your taxation is subject to the whims of other mutual fund shareholders. When these further mutual shareholders panic in a market drop, they force the mutual fund company to sell their profitable positions. In a fast-moving market, these mutual fund company managers must try and do this as tax-efficiently as possible. However, this is very difficult to do in a fast-moving market. What ends up happening is you get stuck with a tax bill because of other (idiot) people's actions. The mutual fund manager will be forced to sell his profitable positions, creating both short and long-term capital gains. If you are one of the mutual fund shareholders who stay put, you are left holding the capital gains tax bag. This means that you have **no control** over the taxation aspect of mutual funds. With ETFs, it does not matter if other shareholders panic and sell. As an ETF shareholder, what other shareholders do is of no concern to you because you have your own cost basis that is unaffected by other shareholders' whims. This is the significant taxation difference between mutual funds and ETFs.

Why invest in mutual funds? Unfortunately, you do not have a choice sometimes. For example, mutual fund companies have a lock on the 401(k) market. It is simply more efficient to trade once per day in a mutual fund at the end of the day, rather than having a 401(k) holding ETFs that can trade all day long. The administration of all those ETF trades would be an administrative nightmare, so mutual funds are the choice for 401(k)s.

When putting together a mutual fund portfolio, you should choose the asset classes as described in the Exchange-Traded Funds chapter. Our mutual fund investment table would look like this:

Large-Cap Stocks	0%
Mid-Cap Stocks	0%
Small-Cap Stocks	0%
Developed Markets Stocks	0%
Emerging Markets Stocks	0%
Ultra-Short-term	0%
Short-term Bonds	0%
Intermediate-term Bonds	0%
Long-term Bonds	0%
High Yield Bonds	0%
Sovereign Debt Bonds	0%
International Bonds	0%
Emerging Market Bonds	0%
Alternatives/Sectors	0%
Cash or Cash Equivalents	0%

Depending on your risk level, in other words, how much to tilt towards stocks will determine how much is left over for fixed income or bonds and cash. Spread your 50% — 75% in stocks across those categories listed above, and the balance spread across the bonds and cash. If you spread your dollars, with spread being the keyword here, then you cannot mess this up. In fact, by spreading asset class dollars, I would probably have a 15% limit in any one particular asset class on the upside and a 5% limit on the minimum investment side. You may want to take my table, make a spreadsheet, and play around with the percentages. For example, create your own model portfolios! Make one that is aggressive, moderately aggressive, moderate, moderately conservative, and conservative. This exercise will help you fine-tune your mutual fund portfolio.

Love them or leave them. Mutual funds are here to stay.

CHAPTER EIGHT

US Government Bonds

Really? You want to know about government bonds? You are kidding, right? Okay. Okay. I will give you a synopsis of government bills, bonds, and notes, but you will not like it when it is all said and done. However, this is good to know information.

The US Treasury sells securities to individuals directly at https://www.treasurydirect.gov.

Treasury bills are issued for less than one year. These Treasury bills are sold at a discount, and when they mature, they pay the face value of the T-bill. The difference is your interest earnings. You can purchase a T-bill for as little as $100. Mainly, they are sold in 4, 8, 13, 26, and 52-week terms. T-bills would fall under the US government bond category from an asset class perspective, then further divided down to the ultra-short-term category.

The next step up in maturities is Treasury notes or T-notes. They are issued in terms of 2, 3, 5, 7, and 10 <u>years</u>. You can also buy a T-note for as little as $100. T-notes pay interest <u>every six months</u> until maturity. The price of a T-note will fluctuate based on the number of years until maturity. The closer to maturity, then the less fluctuation you will experience. The farther away from maturity, then the more fluctuation you will experience. If you do not hold to maturity, you could lose money if you choose to sell early.

Conversely, depending on the interest rate environment, you can also make money by selling early. How you will know is to look at the price. If it is over $100 par value, it is trading at a premium. If it is under $100 par value, it is trading at a discount. At maturity, it simply pays the $100 par value. It is sold at $100 par value for new issues, but if you buy them after they are issued, they could be higher or lower than the par value. These T-notes fall into the short-term and intermediate-term asset class categories.

Treasury bonds or T-bonds are issued in maturities of 20 or 30 years (long-term bonds). They also pay interest every six months. They trade similarly to T-notes in that they trade at either a discount or a premium to the $100 par value. If you sell early, which there is no restriction to do so, you may profit or lose money on your original investment. Most investors hold to maturity on the short and intermediate-term issues (T-bills and T-notes) but typically trade in and out of the T-bonds. Depending on the years to maturity, that will tell you where it falls in your asset class category.

T-bills would fall in the ultra-short-term US government asset class category. The two or 3-year T-notes would fall in the US government short-term asset class. The 5, 7, or 10-year T-notes would fall into the US government intermediate-term asset class. The 20 and 30-year T-bonds would fall into the US government long-term asset class.

The current range of interest for T-bills, T-notes, and T-bonds is roughly 0.03% to 0.90%. This is nothing to write home to grandma about, but sometimes, we need to be safe. US government-issued T-bills, T-notes, and T-bonds are that kind of place, a safe place.

But wait. There are more securities to choose from, including Treasury Inflation-Protected Securities or TIPS. Do you think interest rates are going up? Then, TIPS may be for you. However, they come with a caveat. They are issued in maturities of 5, 10, and 30 years. Now, let me ask you. Which maturity is going to have more volatility? You know the answer. The 30-year maturity will have more volatility. You will see more movement around par value with TIPS that have 30-year maturities as opposed to TIPS that have 5-year maturities. The caveat is the price of 30-year maturities can experience the same shocks to the market as regular 30-year T-bonds, or corporate bonds, for that matter. So, do not be lulled into thinking that just because rates are rising that you will be okay with 30-year TIPS. They get crushed on the par value or price side when rates are rising, but the interest they pay helps offset that crush. I have seen them lose money in a rising interest rate environment, so do not believe they are risk-free. These TIPS also pay interest every six months, but their interest is based on the Consumer Price Index. The major attraction with TIPS is that if interest rates increase (CPI), then your interest will also increase. You need to understand that two things fluctuate regarding TIPS. The interest rate will fluctuate based on the CPI, up or down. In addition, the TIPS price will fluctuate over or under its par value as it gets closer to maturity or farther away from maturity.

There are three other investments that you can purchase from Treasury Direct. These are Floating Rate Notes (FRNs), Series I Savings Bonds, and Series EE Savings Bonds. I am not crazy about any of these, but I will briefly provide an overview of each.

FRNs are issued for a term of two years and pay varying amounts of interest quarterly instead of T-notes and T-bonds that pay every six months. Their interest rates are based on the 13-week T-bill auction. All these investments are "auctioned" to individuals and institutions. Auction is another way to say that they are available for sale. The attraction with an FRN is that if you are in an increasing interest rate environment, then you will have the potential for higher interest rates than a standard 2-year T-note. For example, if you bought a 2-year T-note, then six months later, interest rates went up substantially, you would not get the advantage of the increase in interest rates. However, if you owned a 2-year FRN, then you would. Do you see?

Series I Bonds are 30-year bonds issued in increments of $50, $100, $200, $500, $1,000, and $5,000. Essentially, you purchase the bonds at a discount. Then at maturity, you receive the face amount. These Series I Bonds combine a fixed rate and an inflation rate. Today's Series I Bonds combined rate is 1.68% for a 30-year bond. Hence my reasons for the first paragraph of this chapter. Who would want to buy these things?

Series EE Bonds are guaranteed to double in value if held for 20 years. If you buy a $25 Series EE Bond, then at the 20th year, it will be worth $50. You can hold them up to 30 years, and they will pay interest from 20 years to 30 years. However, the current rate for these Series EE Bonds is 0.10%. Again, that is not anything to write home to grandma about.

Now you know why I believe US government bonds have almost no place in your diversified asset allocation portfolio. You are better off in corporate bonds.

CHAPTER NINE

US Government Agencies

Mortgage-backed bonds are called agencies because they are bonds backed by government agencies such as FNMA (Fannie Mae), FHLMC (Freddie Mac), GNMA (Ginnie Mae), or the VA (Veterans Administration). UMBS is an acronym for residential mortgages backed by Fannie Mae and Freddie Mac that are combined into one security solution that pays interest on a 55-day delay schedule. The official name is Uniform Mortgage-Backed Securities. UMBS's have varying maturities of 10, 15, 20, and 30 years. Have you ever borrowed from a bank, purchased a house, then received notification that your loan has been assigned to another lender? This is typical with residential mortgages because they are packaged together as a UMBS and sold in the fixed income market mainly to institutional investors. Each mortgage inside a mortgage-backed ETF or mutual fund is made up of a combination of residential mortgages (i.e., UMBS's and other agencies). These residential mortgages are segmented by credit scores. Some banks or lenders will sell off the lower credit ones at a discount to other lenders and then keep the higher credit residential loans. This kind of horse-trading goes on all the time with residential mortgages. There is a considerable amount of turnover with residential mortgage-backed securities. During periods of declining interest rates, people with higher interest mortgages tend to refinance. This means that the lender holding that mortgage will not receive the higher interest rate on the original loan. Therefore, they can lose income on these residential mortgage loans. If they lose income, then guess who else loses income? You!

There are also other more complex securities related to mortgages like Collateralized Mortgage Obligations, but I would be getting into the weeds describing CMOs. You will not or should not be buying a CMO anyway, so what is the point of doing a deep dive into how they work?

My apologies, but I digressed. Other ways these mortgage-backed ETFs and mutual funds can lose money is by people defaulting on their loans. During periods of stress in the economy and job layoffs, sometimes people can no longer pay their mortgage payments. Now the lender must spring into action, negotiate the payments, or decide to foreclose on the property. Both cost money and negatively impact a pool of residential mortgages held inside mortgage-backed ETFs and mutual funds. When the default rate goes up, you lose money in your ETF or mutual fund. Banks will often be flexible with a loan default because it is the same as if you bought a stock and it declined 20%. You only lose that 20% if you sell. The same thing goes for the bank. They only lose if they sell the defaulted home loan for a loss.

Here is a little inside baseball on the differences between when a bank will sell a defaulted home loan and when they will hold on to it. What if you lost your job and you had been steadily paying down your mortgage, and you only owe $50,000 on a $300,000 loan. Yet, your monthly mortgage to this bank is $1,645, and you cannot pay it because you lost your job. The bank will snap up your home in a heartbeat. It is simply tough luck for you. You get no credit from the bank for paying down your money early. Why would they do this? Because they have no resale risk to sell your home. You have already paid $250,000 plus interest. If the bank seizes your foreclosure home, they own the home with only a $50,000 balance. They can easily sell it, keep the $250,000 that you already paid, and then get another probably $350,000, pay off the remaining $50,000 at closing because the property appreciated while you were paying down the mortgage. They will earn your $250,000 plus another net of $300,000 to seize your home. ($550,000) They have nothing to lose in this foreclosure example.

Now, let's look at why **you should NEVER pay off your mortgage by paying the money over and above your mortgage payment to your mortgage lender**. Suppose with the same $300,000 loan, instead of paying down the mortgage, you just made the payments, then were laid off. The balance on your mortgage after a year and a half (when you were laid off) is $283,000 or so. Also, assume that your home's price has not appreciated at all during that year and a half. It is still only worth around $300,000. The bank has only received $17,000 or so on the loan. If they were to sell it, the closing costs would be easily over $20,000, so they would lose money by selling it. Therefore, in this situation, the bank would be more apt to work with you on the loan. The moral of this story is to think long and hard about how stable your income is before beginning on a quest to pay off your mortgage. If you have paid it way down and get laid off, then you are screwed.

A better idea would be to invest the money in an investment account **instead of** giving it to the bank to pay down the mortgage. When you have built up the money to pay off the mortgage then, pay it off from your investment account that you had control of the whole time. Do you see? Plus, if you get laid off, you have a fund that you can access to help you through. This is not so if you pay the bank the extra mortgage payment. When you pay extra on the mortgage, it is dead money that you cannot quickly get to when you find yourself in a pinch. Try going to the bank and getting a home equity line of credit after you just got laid off. It is simply not going to happen. Now you know why people hate banks. By the way, did you know that banks can reduce or even eliminate your home equity line of credit? Do not feel too confident about that HELOC always being there because they can yank it out from under you when you need it most. I have seen it happen.

If you invest the money you would have used to pay down the house in an investment account, then guess what? You have emergency funds to keep paying your mortgage! By the way, if you put it in your house, then your return is only the interest rate on the loan. If your loan is 4%, then your return by paying down the mortgage is only 4%, as opposed to investing it in a brokerage account where you have an opportunity to make more than 4%. **This is the only way you should pay down your mortgage**. With a side fund that **you control** in case, you get laid off. This makes a whole lot better sense, in my opinion. I hope you can see the significant differences in my explanation.

Now, back to explaining agencies. I looked at the performance of a popular mortgage-backed ETF for the last ten years, and this was the result. For the calendar year 2020, the return was 3.80%. For the prior three years, it was 3.60% annually. For the preceding five years, it was 2.90% annually, and for the last ten years, the performance was 2.87% per year. Are you excited now? Are you going to run out and buy a mortgage-backed ETF or mutual fund? I doubt it. I would not put them in my diversified portfolio either if I were you.

I am not a fan of agencies. I think I would rather sit in one of those circles and listen to Joe Biden lose his place reading from a teleprompter. How do you lose your place reading from a teleprompter? You can when you have early-onset dementia. I have seen this type of behavior in my own family. Just like your family, people in my family have had dementia-related issues, but we did not prop them up to be President of the United States. It is sad to watch what people with a lust for power will do. I would be surprised if he finishes his four-year term as the PINO. It is Weekend at Bernie's in the White House these days. Except it is not Bernie. They cheated him again!

CHAPTER TEN

Corporate Bonds

Corporations issue corporate bonds. Whew, that was tough to figure out, wasn't it? I know. I am a smart aleck, and nobody likes a smart aleck.

Rating agencies, primarily Fitch, Moody's, and S&P, rate these corporate bonds according to their scale of AAA, AA, A, BBB, BB, B, CCC, CC, C, D, or NR (not rated). Moody's rating service only goes from Aaa down to C. They do not have D or NR ratings. Further, they rate corporate bonds very similar to S&P and Fitch but change the alphabet soup a little, so you know it is a Moody's rated corporate bond. Their alphabet soup is Aaa, Aa, A, Baa, Ba, B, Caa, Ca, and C. Even though Moody's alphabet soup is a little different, overall, it is very similar to S&P and Fitch. Sometimes these firms add a + or - to a rating, like BBB+ or CCC- to indicate they may be raising or lowering their rating soon.

Let me "circle back" here and mention that all US government-issued securities are rated AAA. Only corporations <u>with very strong balance sheets</u> are rated AAA. The rest falls on the scale somewhere. They say AAA, AA, A, and BBB are <u>investment-grade corporates</u>, or Aaa, Aa, A, and Baa if you prefer Moody's ratings. Everything below BBB or Baa is considered **junk** (high yield) bonds.

Remember, we are trying to build a diversified ETF or perhaps mutual fund portfolio, and we want to consider corporate bonds for our asset class categories. What are the asset class categories for corporate bonds? Ultra-short-term, short-term, intermediate-term, long-term, and high yield. ETFs and mutual funds invest in each of these asset class categories. Also, there are ETFs and mutual funds that invest primarily in investment-grade corporates, high-yield corporates, or a mix of differing maturities and ratings. In building your asset class selection utilizing corporate bonds, we want to fill this table.

Ultra-Short-term Corporate Bonds	0%
Short-term Corporate Bonds	0%
Intermediate-term Corporate Bonds	0%
Long-term Corporate Bonds	0%
High Yield Corporate Bonds	0%

Of course, if you want to be more conservative and interest rates are increasing, you would put the bulk of your corporate bond ETF or mutual fund dollars in the ultra-short-term, short-term, and intermediate-term asset classes. If you wanted to be more aggressive, you would add long-term and high yield. A middle-of-the-road approach would be to spread your allocation across all of these. However, you must "circle back" and remember a couple of other fixed-income categories, such as international, sovereign, and emerging market bonds. This means that when you are using up your fixed-income dollars, do not forget that you need to put some dollars to work in these areas, too.

In the corporate bond area, you can buy investment grade only if you are so inclined. Further, you can buy short-term high yields instead of long-term high yields. So, you can do things to reduce your risk in the corporate bond area. There are ETFs and mutual funds for just about every kind of corporate bond that you can imagine. There is no need to over-think it. Make your decisions and adjust as things like interest rates change.

If you have boo-coo amounts of money, then you can buy individual corporate bonds in your brokerage account. That is if you can beat the multi-billion-dollar institutions to the punch. The odds are that you cannot, so you will be better off building your diversified portfolio with ETFs or mutual funds. Of course, corporate bond dividends are taxable. Municipal bond interest is typically free from federal taxation, which we will discuss next.

CHAPTER ELEVEN

Municipal Bonds

Municipal bonds are issued by municipalities (cities), counties, states, utilities owned by cities, school districts, and other issuers. They are free from federal income taxation. You can only buy them in non-qualified accounts like individual, joint, payable on death, or trust accounts. You cannot buy them in IRA or Roth IRA accounts.

You can buy them in the same asset class categories as US government and corporate bonds from an asset class perspective. Ultra-short-term, short-term, intermediate-term, and long-term. There are high-yield municipals, too. The high yield munis are from areas hurting for money and with poor credit ratings. Poor credit ratings usually have to do with mismanagement of some kind, like liberal and progressive politicians spending too much money and not having the tax revenue to compensate. As a result, they go out into the muni market to raise funds. The only thing is they must pay higher interest rates than high-quality munis. You are risking default with these high-yield munis for the little bit of extra yield that they may pay you. Never fear however as I am sure the PINO, Nancy Pelosi and Charles Schumer will bail them out with new legislation.

Today, most munis are paying little to nothing, but they are tax-free! Or are they? Some municipals are taxable. What? Yes, it is true. Some municipals are taxable. Okay. What is the main thing that I need to know about munis? Well, besides the fact that I have never recommended them in my 33-year career, and they pay little to no interest, I suppose you would want to know the difference between a GO bond and a revenue bond. GO bonds are general obligation bonds meaning that the issuer has taxing authority, and the bond is backed by the full faith and credit of the municipality. Revenue bonds are bonds secured by revenues like sales taxes, fuel taxes, school mill taxes, hotel taxes, and utilities. For example, your local utility company may need to put up some new utilities lines or bury some lines, which takes a lot of money. Therefore, the local utility will issue revenue bonds to pay for it and use its customers' utility bills to pay back the bondholders.

How does a 30 year GO bond paying 1.45% sound to you? That's what I thought. Nothing to get excited about, and why on earth would you commit money to something like this? Probably, because you saw an ad on television and you were sold this junk, or excuse me, investment. If you buy individual municipal bonds, you risk more of your money than you would if you purchased a muni bond ETF or mutual fund. Personally, I would not buy muni bond ETFs or muni-bond mutual funds. If you want to add a little tax-free income to your diversified portfolio in a taxable account, then go for it. See that psychiatrist after you do because you have obviously lost your marbles.

CHAPTER TWELVE

Foreign Bonds

To round out your diversified portfolio, you want to add other fixed-income categories such as emerging markets bonds, sovereign bonds, or developed market (international) bonds. Emerging market bonds are issued by emerging market countries like Brazil, Russia, Egypt, Saudi Arabia, Indonesia, Turkey, the Philippines, and others. Sovereign bonds are issued by countries like France, Germany, Japan, the United Kingdom, and others with higher credit standing. Developed market bonds are typically corporate bonds in other countries usually with investment grade ratings.

The bonds issued by emerging market countries generally have higher coupon yields than sovereign bonds. The developed market bonds will have higher credit quality than emerging market countries but a lower coupon yield. If you prefer to be more conservative with these dollars, then allocate more towards developed market bond ETFs and mutual funds. If you want to be more aggressive, then allocate more towards the emerging market and sovereign ETFs and mutual funds. If you are more middle of the road, then spread your allocation evenly between them. Perhaps, you may want an emerging market, a sovereign, and a developed market ETF or mutual fund. The thing that you want to consider is whether the whole world is in a depression. If so, then investing in emerging markets, sovereign bonds, or developed market ETFs and mutual funds might not be a good idea. However, that is usually a rare scenario like 2008. Most of the time, over the long term, you should be fine investing in all three areas: emerging markets, sovereign bonds and developed market ETFs and mutual funds.

We are getting there. Stick with me, and I will have you with a fully diversified portfolio of either ETFs or mutual funds before you know it.

CHAPTER THIRTEEN

Bank Loan Investments

Bank loan funds are sometimes called floating rate funds. The appeal related to these types of funds is that if interest rates are rising, their interest rate also "floats" or rises along with the hike in interest. There is significantly more to this story, however.

I will not spend a lot of time on this because this is an asset class category that some investors and advisors like to use as a substitute for long-term bonds. The thinking is that with interest rates rising, this will hurt long-term bonds' principal value. Then you can offset that risk with floating rate or bank loan funds. As with everything involved in investing, you must use common sense and be quick on your toes.

Imagine a situation where inflation starts to get out of hand. What I mean by that is if the inflation rate goes higher than 5%. We are currently at 0.3% per month. Anyway, using your common sense, I want you to think about a situation in the economy where inflation is running rampant. Bank loans are in bank loan and floating rate funds. Sometimes they call these bank loans "senior" bank loans. That is comforting, isn't it? That must mean they are safe. Excuse me, do not ever believe that. These bank loan funds have normal turnover, with old loans being paid off and new ones being added to their portfolios.

Also, recall that CD rates rise when interest rates go up. Bank loans to businesses also rise when interest rates go up. Many of these bank loans have escalation clauses (variable rates), which means that if interest rates go up, then the interest rate on the bank loans goes up. Now imagine that you are a businessperson who took out an original bank loan at a low interest rate (so you thought), and then suddenly, because of rampant inflation, the price of your supplies went up. As a businessperson (notice I said person instead of non-binary), you are now in a pickle because this bank loan interest rate, along with the supplies, is killing your profits. What do you do? If you do not have any supplies, then you have nothing to sell. The bank loan tends to be the thing that starts going into default. If you are a bank loan or floating rate fund, your overall default rate will start to creep up, and when it does, that affects the principal. As Rush Limbaugh used to say, "For you folks in Rio Linda," that means to lose money. I miss listening to Rush, by the way. He was a great American Patriot like you, who believed in our founding fathers and the incredible US Constitution. It is a genuinely astonishing document, too. It is, without a doubt, the best constitution in the world.

Here is the thing about these bank loan and floating-rate loan funds. When interest rates are rampant, they become significantly, not a little bit, but substantially more at risk. Do not fall for the sales pitch that this is the best place to put money when interest rates are rising. Of course, if you have a diversified ETF or mutual fund portfolio, you should minimize your exposure to this asset class anyway. My point here is to go in with your eyes wide open if you go in at all. These investments take a lot of analysis to fully understand their risks.

CHAPTER FOURTEEN

CD's

Certificates of Deposit or CDs are issued by banks and pay a guaranteed amount of interest. As of today, there are CDs available that pay 0.02%. Yes, you read that correctly. I remember when CDs paid double digits when I was a young whippersnapper. Of course, back then, Jimmy Carter was the President, and he made some poor decisions that caused most of the problems. That is no slam on the guy since he has done more for people with his Habitat for Humanity charity than most people will ever do in their lifetime. However, if you like Mr. Carter or not, this one period has had more influence than just about anything else in American history. That sounds overly dramatic, but the underlying issue back then was runaway inflation. When inflation went to new heights, this caused significant problems to the US economy. Ever since the early 1980s, the Federal Reserve and economists have been deathly scared of inflation returning to those heights. It will never happen again, in my opinion. Today we have a Federal Reserve Board of Governors who is only too happy to throw a wet blanket on the US economy by raising rates. I do not even like it when these people talk to the media. It seems like every time they do, they are sounding some alarm, thus impacting the stock market negatively. Today, the Federal Reserve Chairman talked, and the Dow Jones Industrial Average is off over 400 points, proving my point. They just need to do their job and shut up!

CDs are so simple that there is not much to talk about with them. The only thing that I would offer is that you can buy FDIC insured CDs from multiple banks in your brokerage account. Instead of driving all over town and opening CDs at different banks, you can simply buy several CDs in your brokerage account, if so inclined.

Of course, CDs are insured up to $250,000 to protect investor savings. Today, I looked at the CD rates, which I found a 3-month CD is paying 0.02 to 0.05%, but it is guaranteed! A 1-year CD is paying 0.05 to 0.1%. You can get a five-year CD for up to .50%. All of these are nothing to write home to grandma about but could be a place to temporarily park some cash until you decide how to invest it.

CDs and cash equivalents fit the *cash* asset class in your diversified or focus portfolio. Conversely, CDs are not immune from crashing and burning, either. In the early 1980s, there were several Savings & Loans that offered CDs that crashed and burned. They were buying junk bonds back then. When interest rates went up to double digits, it made it almost impossible for the junk bond issuers to pay those high-interest rates, so they simply defaulted. When they defaulted, the Savings & Loans were left holding the bag. They could not pay those double-digit CD rates. I'm not sure if you noticed, but we no longer have any Savings & Loans anymore. They existed as a place for loaning mortgages to home buyers. They invested their capital in junk bonds, and the house of cards went down when the junk bond market crashed, and people quit paying their mortgages. Lesson learned. Safety in CDs is guaranteed because of FDIC, but if a bank goes down, it could be months and months before you receive your money back.

The recap is that CDs are guaranteed by the FDIC, but I would not be locking up a ton of your money in CDs, if any. This cash and cash equivalents (CDs) asset class just acts as a cushion for when the market goes down, and it will from time to time. If it does, then 2.5% — 10% of your diversified portfolio or focused portfolio will hold up.

CHAPTER FIFTEEN

Money Market Funds

Money market funds are mutual funds with a stable price of $1.00. There are money market funds whose price fluctuates based on the underlying assets today. Most people who own brokerage accounts are familiar with the sweep feature. When you place a trade in your diversified or focused portfolio, then the money to pay for that trade is "swept" from your money market fund. That is why they call them "sweep" funds. Sweep funds today are paying 0.01% and are waiving their expenses. Today, they are a loss leader for most brokerage firms because these fund expenses can range from 0.19 to 0.35% generally. Therefore, by paying 0.01%, they are losing money.

Other money market funds are "non-sweep" and pay higher rates of around 0.03%. A non-sweep money market fund is one that you must place a sell trade to make the cash available. When you compare a three-month CD rate, which has a penalty for early withdrawal, versus a non-sweep money market fund, then you will find the non-sweep money market fund may pay a smidge more interest. However, the tradeoff is that the FDIC does not guarantee the sweep and non-sweep money market funds. This begs the question..." How risky are sweep and non-sweep money market funds?" There has only been one money market fund that I know of that crashed and burned, and that was during the 2008 period. This money market fund crashed and burned because they were doing something they should not have been doing. They were buying investments that were extremely risky and very illiquid, and they had a run on their fund due to the 2008 depression. Those factors caused it to crash and burn because they could not sell their illiquid investments. Otherwise, it is infrequent for a money market fund, sweep or non-sweep, to crash and burn. I would not lose any sleep over it.

CHAPTER SIXTEEN

Currency Funds

Currency funds are another type of cash equivalent that you can invest in. There are investments that hold other countries' currencies like the Euro, the British pound, the Japanese yen, the Canadian dollar, the Swedish krona, the Swiss franc, the Australian dollar, and the Chinese Yuan. All these currencies move in relation to the US dollar. In effect, you are making a bet that one nation's currency will outperform the US dollar. You must think of these funds like money market funds in foreign countries holding investments in their native currency. If they are money market funds, then the returns will be like money market funds. However, because they fluctuate in price based on the underlying currency, then there are rare opportunities to make 1 to 3% if you trade in and out of them.

In several European countries, they are actually paying negative interest in order to discourage people from parking their cash. Believe it or not, Europeans are still parking their cash even though they are losing money. Go figure.

The problem with investing in currencies is your knowledge of the Chinese Yuan, for example. More than likely, you have no knowledge of the Chinese Yuan. Therefore, it would not be too smart to invest in a currency fund based on the Chinese Yuan. I just wanted to briefly explain currency funds if you were curious about another way to lose your money.

CHAPTER SEVENTEEN

Stock Options

I put this chapter here for the curious. However, it **is not** appropriate for a diversified or focused portfolio unless you want to put on some **covered calls** and make a little extra income. Therefore, you may want to skip this chapter unless you are a glutton for punishment. Otherwise, if you always wanted to know something about options trading, then read on, my friend.

Options are difficult for most people to understand, but rest assured, I will make it as simple as possible. I am a former Series 9 and 10, which means that I supervised all the option trades in my brokerage office when I held these licenses. I do not have these licenses anymore because I want nothing to do with being employed by a brokerage firm. With all the "office politics, back-stabbing and lying," corporate America is not the place that I want to be. Even though I was an options supervisor, there still is a lot to understand about options. In my mind, there is an easy explanation about how they work, but the hard part is being right when you make your buy and sell decisions. Plus, finding a bargain in option chain prices is very difficult to accomplish, but I will "circle back" to this later.

Let's start with the easy part. I want you to think of a seesaw that you played on when you were a kid. One side goes up, and one side goes down. This is the way options work. If you **buy** a CALL on a stock, you are betting that the stock price will go up, hit your strike price, and then everything over that will be your profit minus the cost of the CALL. If you **sell** a CALL on a stock, you are betting the opposite, that the stock will not go up or hit your strike price, and then you will receive the income from the CALL or the CALL premium. Do you see how simple that is? Of course, I am facetious.

Let's "circle back" here for a moment. What is the strike price? Oh, my dear friend, this is where you must place your bets. Let me give you an example. Suppose you think XYZ stock is going to the moon and you want to buy a CALL on it. XYZ is currently trading at $100 per share, and you are looking for a CALL strike price of $110 per share before options expiration in three months. Don't worry. I will "circle back" to this options expiration thing in a bit. Anyway, so you look up the CALL option price for a $110 strike price that expires in three months, and you find that this particular CALL option is trading at $4. (You multiply the $4 by $100 to get what it will cost per 100 shares.) What is your breakeven? Well, you are sure XYZ is going to the moon, right? The price of $110 is going to happen for sure in your mind. It should blow right past that in the next three months. Otherwise, you would not be buying this CALL option. Your breakeven is $114, which is the $110 strike price plus the cost of your $4 CALL option. You are sure XYZ is going to the moon, so this is not a problem.

Now, we can look at what happens when it fails to reach your strike price, when it almost reaches your strike price and when it exceeds your strike price. If it fails to reach $110, then at the end of three months, you lose the price you paid, which is the $400 per CALL option. Your total loss depends on how many CALL options you bought at the $4 strike price. Each CALL option costs $100 per strike price, so if you had five contracts with a strike price of $4, then your all-in loss is $2,000 ($4 x $100 x 5).

What if XYZ stock ends up at $112 at the end of three months? Well, in this case, you lose $2 on each of your CALL options. That is better than losing $4 per contract. If you had 5 CALL options, then you would lose $1,000 ($2 x $100 x 5). There are per contract charges that differ by the brokerage firm, so I am leaving those charges out of this example.

The choice you want is where XYZ's price goes to the moon in three months. Suppose XYZ is priced at $120 at the end of three months. Your profit would be $120 - $110 - $4, or a $6 per CALL option profit. Remember that you have to multiply the CALL times 100, so your price to buy the CALL option was not $4, but rather $400 times the number of CALL options you bought. It is easier to explain before you factor in that important detail. Your profit in this example was $6 ($600) per CALL option times the 5 contracts which equals $3,000 ($6 x $100 x 5).

You can think of buying CALL options as another way to earn the appreciation of a stock that you like without all of the outlay. I will use Amazon as an example. Today, 100 shares of Amazon is priced at $2,995, so if you wanted to own 500 shares, then your cost would be $1,497,500. Yes. You read that correctly. Now, I have a question for you. If you wanted to own Amazon and were sure it was going to the moon, plus you could risk $2,000 to buy 5 CALL(s), then your cost would be $2,000 as opposed to $1,497,500. Of course, you do not own Amazon. You own the right to exercise Amazon CALL options at a price you believe it will exceed before expiration. In a way, it is a poor man's way to profit on stocks (Buying a CALL). However, you can lose all of your premium to buy a CALL, and you do not own the stock. Of course, I was just using that as an example. Amazon call options are much more expensive than $4 per contract.

Now, I wanted to "circle back" to option chains (pricing). The actual price of an Amazon CALL right now will dissuade you from buying CALL options. For example, if we go 107 days out, we will find that to buy an Amazon CALL with a strike price of $3,040, it will cost you $214.50 per contract or $21,450 per hundred shares. Yikes! If you bought five contracts, then it would cost you $107,250 for the privilege of Amazon rising in price from $2,995 to $3,040, barely a 1.5% return. Huh? You read that right. Now you know why most people do not buy CALL(s) but instead sell covered calls for the income when they already own the stock. By selling 5 Amazon CALL(s) in my example, then you get the premium of $107,250 if Amazon does not rise to $3,040. However, you should see the risk in selling CALL options, too. Amazon only has to increase 1.5%, and you lose all of that premium and have to give up your Amazon stock in my example. It is a seesaw that can swing both ways. Do you see? You will spend countless hours looking for bargains in option chains and probably never find one, but occasionally people get lucky.

If you are betting that XYZ stock's price is going to the moon, then there is also someone on the other side who is betting it is not going to the moon. We can look at this opposite position scenario now. Instead of buying a CALL option, we are selling a CALL option. I will "circle back" to PUT options in a bit. We can use the same numbers for example purposes. If you sell a CALL on XYZ at $110, you are betting that XYZ's price will not reach $110 in the next three months. The CALL strike price that you are selling is the same $4 ($400). Now, we can look at our three scenarios on this side of the seesaw. If XYZ's price stays below $110, you get to keep the $4 ($400) per contract. If we had 5 contracts, then our profit is $2,000 ($4 x $100 x 5). This is what you want as a seller of CALL options. Our next scenario is when XYZ's price goes to $112 at the end of our three months, so our CALL option will get exercised (closed out). We will either have to pay $2 ($200) per contract or deliver 100 shares of the stock of XYZ times the number of CALL options that we were selling. In other words, if we had five contracts of XYZ $110 CALL options that we were selling, then we would have to hand over 500 shares of XYZ stock or pay the loss of $2 ($200) per contract, or $1,000 ($2 x $100 x 5). If in our final scenario, the price of XYZ blew through $110 and went to $120, then we would have to deliver 500 shares of XYZ in our five contract example and lose our $4 premium. Of course, in most cases, the seller of CALL options already owns the 500 shares of stock, so they just hand over their 500 shares of stock at exercise. Sellers of CALL options are okay with their stock being exercised because it means that the 500 shares of stock that they owned had a profit when it was exercised. They could have purchased that XYZ stock originally at $80 per share, and therefore, even though it got exercised, they received a long-term capital gain of $30 per share ($110 strike price). These are called **covered call** options, where you sell a CALL against stock that you already own and that you are okay with it being exercised. By the way, this is probably the most favored options trading strategy: selling a CALL against your current stock holding. In most cases, you receive the premium unless the stock goes to the moon, then you do not.

Recapping the buyer of a CALL option wants the stock price to exceed the strike price, and the seller of a CALL wants the stock to flounder and not exceed the strike price. The buyer makes money if the CALL option exceeds the strike price and the option's cost. The CALL option's seller keeps the premium of the option if the stock doesn't reach the strike price. Do you see why I call it a seesaw?

Now, let's "circle back" to PUT options. We still have our same XYZ stock with a strike price of $110 and $4 ($400) per contract. We have to think inversely with PUT options, but we still have the seesaw. A PUT option buyer wants the price to go below the strike price. For example, let's give XYZ a current price of $120 per share. The PUT buyer wants XYZ to go below $110, the strike price, and is paying $4 ($400) per contract. Now, let's look at our three scenarios on the put side. If XYZ's price goes to $100 per share, our buy PUT option is profitable, and our profit would be $110 - $100 or $10 per contract minus the price we paid for the PUT option, which is $4 ($400) per contract. Our net profit is $10 minus $4 = $6. If we had five contracts, our profit is 5 x $6 x $100 per contract price, or $3,000 total.

If XYZ's price ended up at the end of three months at $108, which is $2 less than the strike price, then we essentially get $2 of our $4 cost of buying the PUT option in return. Of course, our final scenario is where the price of XYZ stays above $110, then our purchased PUT option expires worthless, and we lose our $4 ($400) per contract. All you risk as a buyer of a PUT option is your premium.

As I mentioned earlier, like with the CALL options, there is a seesaw with PUT options. In other words, there is someone on the other side of the transaction. A seller of a PUT option is betting that the price of XYZ will not go below the strike price of $110 per share. Again, looking at our three scenarios for the seller of a PUT option, we can find that the seller makes money if XYZ's price stays above the $110 strike price. If it goes to $108, then the seller of the PUT option loses $2 ($200) per contract. If XYZ's price goes down to $100 per share, then the PUT option seller has to come up with the $10 per share difference, plus they lose the cost of the PUT option, which was $4 ($400) in our example. So, this seller of this PUT option is out $10 ($1,000) times the number of contracts which in our example was 5, so they are out $5,000. The risk to a seller of PUT options is, in our example, a drop from $120 down to $110. That is the maximum loss unless they do not own the stock to cover it, which is called selling naked put options. When you **sell naked put options**, you have to cover the other side of the seesaw, which means they have to buy 500 shares of the stock while the stock could be tanking in price. As a result, you could lose more than $10 if you are on margin. When you multiply that times five contracts, then yikes! If you do not have the 500 shares in your brokerage account, then that is why it is called naked. It is a significant potential loss if you have to buy 500 shares and do not already own the 500 shares. I do not want you to worry. The odds of your brokerage firm giving you this top option level is slim-to-none.

The above section is a basic understanding of CALL and PUT options. There are other ways of utilizing options like spreads and straddles, but I will not explain those because that takes specialized expertise and experience, and your brain would go into a deep fog. These are essentially ways of buying a PUT and a CALL simultaneously to protect stock positions and gain a little income at the same time. Besides, we would be getting in the weeds if I did explain spreads and straddles. I would rather watch Joe Biden fall down three times trying to walk up Air Force One's stairs rather than explain spreads and straddles. Ouch! I like to keep it simple if there is such a thing in understanding options. I was confused just writing this. I can imagine how you feel.

Now, I would like to let you know that there are <u>restrictions</u> on who can trade options and who cannot. Supposedly, it is for your own protection, but who knows why they make these rules? There are 2, 4, or 5 levels of option approvals for people who trade options typically. It depends on the brokerage firm and whether you are trading stock or ETF options or trading index options. For example, Fidelity has 5 Levels, and Schwab has 4 Levels. Fidelity labels theirs Levels 1 - 5. Schwab labels theirs Levels 0 - 3. Robinhood has Level 2 and Level 3. Again, do not ask me why? I guess it is like the difference between Ford and GM, but again, who knows?

With Fidelity, you can see for yourself at https://www.fidelity.com/options-trading/start-trading-options. At Schwab, you can visit https://www.schwab.com/options. With Robinhood, you can visit https://robinhood.com/us/en/support/articles/options-knowledge-center/. You may be a TD Ameritrade fan and know about their sophisticated options trading platform and authority levels to do options trading. Schwab purchased TD Ameritrade recently, and they are going to become one firm sometime soon. As far as options trading is concerned, I guess that they will probably use Schwab's options trading levels or tweak them a little when they add TD Ameritrade. TD Ameritrade has excellent software, too. Your guess, however, is as good as mine as to what ends up being Schwab's options trading policy after the merger of the two companies. Here is a link to the TD Ameritrade options page on their website. https://www.tdameritrade.com/investment-products/options-trading.html.

If you want to learn more, go to one of the above websites for more information. I do not want to be any more redundant than I am already.

When you are trading options, you also need a margin account. Each of the above firms charges different margin interest rates. If you have bad credit, you can probably forget about doing much, if any, options trading, except the elementary stuff like covered calls. These firms' margin interest rate ranges from as low as 2.5% to as high as 9.5%. Again, I am not making any recommendations.

Here is the bad news. Just because you want to trade options does not mean that you can trade options. Huh? You have to **get approval from your brokerage firm,** and they assign a level to your trading account. If you have never traded options before, then you can count on a pretty basic trading ability like selling a call (covered calls) when you hold the stock already. Your brokerage firm can deny even something mundane as buying a call for cash. You may be wondering how do you get the ability to do the upper levels in options trading? Beats me. Remember when I said that I used to supervise options approvals for my brokerage firm's clients? When I applied with that experience, I was only given Level 1 with Schwab. I called them to complain but to no avail. Since I did not have a verifiable recent trading history, they assigned me Level 1 even though I used to sign off on all options applications! Go figure. Therefore, as I said earlier, just because you want to trade options doesn't mean that you can trade options. Although, I will say that some firms are more generous than others with their option levels.

Trading options is a complicated strategy and not for the faint at heart. Now that you know some basics about options, you can now learn the sad truth about option pricing chains. Suppose you believe XYZ stock is going to the moon and you want to buy a CALL option at $110 when the stock is currently trading at $100. I used a per contract price of $4 per contract in my example above. However, it all depends on the stock, my friend. If you want to trade options on a trendy stock, then everybody and their brother may have the same idea as you. This means that instead of $4 per contract, it might be $16 or even $160 per contract. Oh, I see said the blind man. The cost of trading options just went up. Trust me. You will spend countless hours looking at option chain pricing and discover that there are no bargains unless you beat everyone else to the punch. The goal is to keep the premiums or protect your losses with options trading. If it costs too much to do that, or you have to risk too much, then what is the point? Go ahead and price some options and come back and tell me that I am wrong.

Now, I want to "circle back" to options expiration choices. My example above was three months, but you can go out six months, nine months, a year, two years, or even three years on your options. More decisions for you are ahead based on what you think your favored stock will do after hitting your strike price and paying or receiving the premium. The shorter options expiration periods are generally the more expensive ones. The longer-term options expiration dates are usually, not always, but typically having less costly premiums. I told you this stuff was complicated.

Okay. That is enough about options. I would rather listen to a Jen Psaki press conference counting all the "um's" and "circle backs" than go through that again. You are on your own when it comes to option trading.

CHAPTER EIGHTEEN

Alternatives

What are alternatives? These are investments that you can buy (and sell) with a specific focus. An example of this would be leveraged and inverse funds. These funds are hazardous and are only meant to be held one day. However, most investors in this area do not follow that recommendation and keep them for way too long.

There are three types of inverse funds. Short 1x, short 2x, or short 3x their underlying asset class or index. You can also buy (leveraged) up 1x, up 2x, and up 3x the underlying asset class or index. Suppose you look at the S&P 500® index and decide to short it. You can short it 1x, 2x, or even 3x, but you need to understand the math. If you invested in a 3x Short S&P 500® and the S&P 500® declined 2%, then the way these are supposed to work is your Short 3x should make 6%. However, **it seldom happens**. I have seen instances of this scenario and the 3x only earning 1%. Why? Because big institutional trading firms are jumping in and out of these funds with their computer algorithms. Small investors like you get stuck holding the bag. If I were you, then I would stay far away from these types of investments. It is pure gambling, in my opinion. The US Securities and Exchange Commission does not like them either. See for yourself at https://www.investor.gov/introduction-investing/general-resources/news-alerts/alerts-bulletins/investor-alerts/sec-finra. If the SEC is against them, then perhaps you should listen to them.

Another type of alternative is a long/short fund. This is an ETF or mutual fund that buys 130% long positions (stocks the fund manager expects to go up in value) and shorts 30% of what they feel are stocks that they believe are poor performers for the future. The jury is still out on these long/short funds. In my opinion, you are getting a little complicated with your diversified or focused portfolio by using a long/short fund. Why do you want to complicate your life?

Yet another type of alternative investment is managed futures. Managed futures in an ETF or mutual fund make choices for investing in futures for you. Instead of you betting on cotton, oil, pork bellies, copper, index futures, and other things, you hire a managed futures ETF or mutual fund firm to do it for you. In my opinion, there are not enough upside possibilities compared to the more likely downside scenarios. The returns on these have been awful over the last ten years. Again, why do you want to complicate your life?

Yet another type of alternative is a hedge fund. You have probably heard of hedge funds. In the institutional world, there are real hedge funds. In the ETF and mutual fund world, there are hedge replication funds. Hedge replication funds try to mimic or copy what hedge funds are doing. There are several categories of these. I have already discussed some of them, but here are the others. Merger arbitrage, event-driven, fixed-income arbitrage, short-only, market-neutral, convertible arbitrage, credit, global macro, and quantitative. Do you know what any of this means? That is what I thought! I will not explain all of these because it would be a big waste of your and my time but realize this fact. When all the little Robinhood investors decided to buy GameStop and keep buying it and held onto it, the intelligent **short-only** hedge fund managers got their hats handed to them. The moral of the story is that Alternatives are not what hedge fund managers would have you believe. With long-term being the keyword here, their long-term track record is not all that different from their category. Trust me, and do not believe the binary person trying to sell you a hedge fund. Did you catch that?

Binary means male or female, and it drives liberals crazy. Further, our old friend, the Ponzi schemer, often originates as a hedge fund from time to time. Why? Because any Ponzi schemer can raise money from unsuspecting people like you without being registered and flying under the radar. Before you realize what happened, you will be fleeced. This is another area where you have to do a lot of homework to ensure the hedge fund is legit. It is much easier to invest in a hedge replication ETF or mutual fund than have to meet a hedge fund's qualifications, plus absorb all the research on them. Never mind about finding out whether they are licensed or not. Most people do not know how to research or check the license of a hedge fund. Both are scarce and hard to find. The best decision you can make is to only invest in publicly traded investments unless you are rich as all get out. Then, perhaps you could buy a real hedge fund.

Hedge funds are like being a member of the most expensive country club in town. If you can afford it, then you might want to consider it. Otherwise, stick with hedge replication ETFs and mutual funds if you're going to commit some dollars in this area.

CHAPTER NINETEEN

RegD - Private Placements

Regulation D offerings are **unregistered** private placements. This means nobody is watching the store for you folks in Rio Linda, California. There are three versions of RegD offerings. Rule 504, Rule 505, and Rule 506. **A large majority of Ponzi schemes are disguised as RegD offerings**. Private placements or RegD offerings are very risky and may be extraordinarily difficult to sell or recover your original investment.

With **Rule 504**, issuers (private companies) can sell (not you) up to $1,000,000 of securities in any 12 months. These securities are restricted from resale, and if you need quick cash, you can forget it. Often, local businesses and their corporate real estate broker may make a Rule 504 offering to raise money for a business venture. They put in some of their own money, then invite business associates, friends, and family to invest alongside them. All investors in Rule 504 offer a share in the firm's profits and losses.

Rule 505 is where you need to raise as much as $5,000,000 in securities every 12 months to an unlimited number of accredited investors, but no more than 35 non-accredited investors.

> Accredited investors are those with earned income that exceeds $200,000 (single) or $300,000 (married) in the prior two years and reasonably expects to do the same in the current year. Or, they could have a net worth of over $1,000,000, excluding their residence.

Rule **506** is just like Rule 505, except that the non-accredited investors should be sophisticated in financial and business matters. This sophistication can be satisfied by hiring a purchaser representative sophisticated in business and financial issues. For example, an attorney, a CPA, credentialed commercial real estate broker, or someone like me.

When you are trying to build a diversified or focused portfolio, my question is..." Why do you just have to invest in a RegD offering?" Isn't this something that you can live without? There is no need to lock up your money into something **illiquid** that may end up losing money or worse. Unless you are friends with someone like **Peter Thiel**, I would not ever invest in a RegD offering. By the way, one of the best books to read if you are thinking of starting a business is Peter Thiel's book, **Zero to One**. I highly recommend it. The entire business world of startups will make more sense to you, and you will learn not to copy others but rather create a business that no one else is doing. Think hard and long before opening any business that other people are already doing. Read **Zero to One**, if you are thinking of starting a business. In doing so, this will probably save you from a significant mistake.

I wanted you to know about RegD just in case you meet one of the followers of Charles Ponzi. The vast majority of Ponzi schemes are unregistered RegD offerings. I just saved you millions of dollars. Aren't you going to thank me?

CHAPTER TWENTY

SPACs

SPACs or **S**pecial **P**urpose **A**cquisition **C**ompanies are publicly traded companies whose purpose is to invest in, most of the time, their own private companies. Although, other SPACs raise money to target private companies that they want to participate in or buy into. These SPACs supply the money to buy a portion of private companies looking to go public, and when they do, the SPAC will profit (hopefully). Some private companies create their own SPAC instead of going the IPO route. If the SPAC raises enough money for their private company in the public stock markets, they will eventually go public and bypass all the typical IPO costs. The main advantage of a private company that wants to go public is that via the SPAC, they have access to investors who believe in the company and want to invest in it. If the target company does not materialize within a short time frame, typically two years, then all of the investors' money will be returned to them. A regular IPO is time-intensive and comes with significant costs (Wall Street), which they can avoid with the SPAC.

One significant difference between a regular IPO and a SPAC IPO is that the stock market values its price with the typical IPO. With a SPAC, the SPAC management values and prices the SPAC because they trade as warrants. Warrants are rights to buy specific stocks. What should this tell you? It should say to you need a whole lot of confidence in the management team of the SPAC. The US Securities and Exchange Commission has issued an Investor Alert on SPACs due to their recent rise in popularity. You can find it here: https://www.sec.gov/oiea/investor-alerts-and-bulletins/what-you-need-know-about-spacs-investor-bulletin. Like with any other investment, you should do your homework. If the US Securities and Exchange Commission has issued an Investor Alert on SPACs, then you may want to read it.

Read the IPO prospectus of the SPAC and discover why they created it, what private company is being targeted for purchase, and the principal people involved. There is no apples-to-apples comparison you can do with SPACs since they are all formed for a different reason. This could be an area to invest in for your focused or more risky dollars, but you have to do your homework! Read their prospectus! Research the definition of a SPAC. This investment cries out for due diligence.

CHAPTER TWENTY-ONE

Annuities

Annuities fall into the fixed income portion of your diversified portfolio. There are several different types of annuities. Some are simple to understand, and others are complex. The simple one to understand is the fixed annuity. It is like a CD in that it pays a fixed rate of interest for a specified number of years. Wait. CDs are more short-term, aren't they? Yes, while fixed annuities tend to be 3, 5, 7, and even ten-year terms. Today, the three-year rates range from 1.3% to 2.25%, depending on the insurance company. The five-year rates range between 1.9% and 2.7%. The seven-year rates range from 1.9% to 2.8%. The ten-year rates range from 1.95% to 2.6%. Each fixed annuity has a surrender period based on those 3-, 5-, 7-, or 10-year periods. As you may or may not know, annuities grow tax-deferred, but you pay ordinary income taxes on the first dollar you pull out. However, if you **annuitize** your annuity, then there is a calculation called an "exclusion ratio." The exclusion ratio is where they calculate your cost basis and the growth of the annuity and come up with a percentage. For example, if you put in $80,000 and it grew to $100,000 over several years or decades more likely at these low-interest rates, then your exclusion ratio would be 80% non-taxable and 20% taxable. This is the taxation if you **annuitize** the annuity.

If you take a plain old withdrawal from the non-qualified fixed annuity and do not annuitize it, it is taxed based on LIFO. This means that every withdrawal is taxed until you reach your original principal. Using my same $80,000 investment that grows to $100,000 and you make a withdrawal, your first $20,000 would be taxed as ordinary income. Only after you have withdrawn all of your $20,000 in earnings would you get to the tax-free cost basis or principal. Insurance companies do not like to give people their money back, so they try and con you into annuitizing non-qualified annuities. **This is not a good idea in most cases**. Look what they are paying above again and realize that you will never see the principal again when you annuitize your annuity. The insurance company keeps it and is guaranteed to pay you an income stream. (Typical insurance agent sales pitch: "guaranteed income.")

Now, you have to put on your critical thinking cap because I will blow annuitization out of the water here. Suppose you took that $80,000 and invested it in a diversified portfolio. What are the odds that you might make more than those annuity rates described above? You have a pretty good chance at beating 3% over 7 or 10 years. For example, let's assume you were an awful investor, and your $80,000 only grew to $100,000. Now, you are retired and need income. Well, you have $100,000. You can pay yourself an income stream from this money, but the difference is your principal's balance stays invested. In the annuity, **it is gone**. There will be no more opportunity for growth. Your uneducated insurance agent will tell you that their annuity is "guaranteed" while your strategy of investing on your own has stock market risk. Remember, these people have no expertise in professional money management. The odds of you growing your $80,000 to only $100,000 in 10 years is virtually impossible, but for argument's sake, let's go with it. If you stay invested in a diversified portfolio over any ten years, you will make more than 3%. Plus, if you withdrew $5,000 in the first year, $95,000 would **still be invested** earning growth. In the second year, you would pay yourself another $5,000, but since you kept control of your money instead of annuitizing it, and if you earned 5% on it, then your $95,000 would have grown back to $99,750. If you made more than 5%, you would have even more money, and still, you would have paid yourself a 5% income stream. But wait. There is more. You still have your principal, which you can control. This is not true with the annuitized annuity. It is **gone** if you annuitize it. Finally, what about your heirs? With the annuitized annuity, **they receive nothing when you die**. With the invested money you control, they will receive the entire value on a step-up basis (no taxes). Your heirs would only owe taxes on the growth since your date of death, which should be little or nothing because most heirs get those funds within a few months. With the PINO in the White House, who knows how long this step-up in basis thing will hold up, but for now, it is the law.

> "Annuitizing a non-qualified annuity is a **dumb** idea. Buying a fixed annuity may be an even **dumber** idea."

Never fear my friends. Other types of annuities offer a chance at a better return, like fixed indexed annuities and variable annuities. Fixed **indexed** annuities are touted as "stock market returns without the risk." That is a bunch of bunk. Once you understand cap and participation rates, plus market value adjustments, then you will realize that your insurance agent has fooled you. I do not want to go deep into the weeds on fixed indexed annuities, but it is safe to say that their returns are just a smidge over regular fixed annuities. You may be able to make 10% some years, but nothing in others, so you will realize that you made 5% on it long term when you average it out.

Insurance agents like to show you fancy charts against a horrible stock market over, say, ten years. Again, the likelihood of the stock market losing money in any ten years is nil. By golly, the insurance agent trying to sell you that fixed indexed annuity will paint a doom and gloom picture of the stock market and tell you when the stock market goes down, "You will not lose a dime!" Wait a minute. Isn't this fixed indexed annuity based on a stock market index? On the one hand, the insurance agent tells you that you can receive stock market returns without the risk. On the other hand, the agent says that you will be happy to accept zero returns when the stock market goes down, which is better than losing money in the stock market. I'm sorry, but I am confused. Do I want the stock market to do good in this fixed indexed annuity, or should I be happy with zero returns in lousy stock market years? You see what I mean. You cannot have it both ways.

Most insurance agents do not have a lick of sense when investing money. They are the last people on the planet to take investment advice from because they are like liberals who watch fake news. They just follow a **sales script** similar to liberals who cannot think for themselves and just regurgitate what they see on television or read from the fake news media. That is why we heard "there is no evidence of election fraud" so often. Liberals and talking heads just repeated what the mainstream "fake news" media and politicians told them. I honestly believe that there is a daily communication with all the fake news outlets that gives them their daily talking points. Why else would they all say the same thing on every fake news outlet? Do not believe me? Flip the channels from one fake news channel to another and see if you notice if they are talking about the same issues on both fake news channels.

Liberals and progressives are crazy and like to scream at you. If you are a black conservative, they yell at you and call you an Uncle Tom for believing in the US constitution. If you are a white conservative, they call you a racist or white supremacist. Now, they are even telling Asian Americans that they have white privilege. Please! American Patriots do not like these labels. These liberals and progressives are awful people. Whatever they accuse you of doing, they are doing it themselves a lot of times. Right now, there are a bunch of hate crimes against Jewish people going on all over the country. Where is the damn FBI? Boy they sure jumped on the Bubba Wallace fake noose thing, but have no inclination to go after real hate *with violence* no less against Jewish people. Yet for some unexplained reason, a lot of Jewish people vote

Democrat. That is a real head scratcher to me. Where are the Democrats who are standing up for the Jewish people?

Back to my subject. Insurance agents never research anything. They simply follow the insurance company sales pitch. Insurance agents are given promotional material from the insurance company to sell you a fixed indexed annuity. When they pull out the insurance company's glossy marketing materials, then you should look out! Their sales pitch is soon to follow.

The insurance agent makes 6.5% on every sale, by the way. Who does this help first? The insurance company. Who does it help second? The insurance agent. Who gets stuck in the annuity with a ten-year surrender charge? **You**! Ding, ding, ding! Is that alarm bell in your head ringing yet? You can thank me later. I still need to explain variable annuities. The taxation is the same with **fixed** annuities, **fixed indexed** annuities, and **variable** annuities in a non-qualified (taxable) annuity.

Variable annuities are where you can do the best as far as returns on annuities are concerned. Variable annuities have mutual fund company sub-accounts similar to regular mutual funds. You can design a diversified or focused portfolio inside a variable annuity. Now we are getting somewhere. Not so fast. Variable annuities have management expenses which are charges from the insurance company. Plus, the investments (mutual fund sub-accounts) also have management fees. The insurance agent likes to add on riders to these variable annuities in "guaranteed income" roll-ups. For example, they will say this variable annuity is guaranteed at the end of 10 years, to add 7% every year if held for those ten years. In the small type, you will read:

> "You have to annuitize this annuity to get the roll-up."

This fine print is not likely to ever come across your insurance agent's lips. <u>You have to annuitize the variable annuity to get that 7% roll-up</u>. Uh oh! We already learned about annuitizing an annuity earlier. It is not good. Again, you can probably make that same 7%

over ten years of investing on your own and **still control the principal**. Duh! These insurance agents are always trying to get your money and **forever, no less**! They want to make outlandish assumptions that will never happen. They want you to give your money to the insurance company where your heirs receive nothing if you annuitize your variable annuity. What a deal! Did I mention that most variable annuities have expenses of 2.5% to as much as 4% or more with riders? I wonder. If I have to overcome a 2.5% to 4% expense ratio over the next ten years, how am I going to make any money on this thing? By the way, there is no downside protection in most variable annuities for your principal. If it loses 20% in the first year because your insurance agent is an idiot and does not know how to build a diversified portfolio, then too bad. Do not forget about the 10% surrender charge in that first year, either. How do you like variable annuities so far? Did that insurance agent tell you that you can buy a variable annuity **without paying them a 6.5% commission** and sticking you with a ten-year surrender charge? Why not? Silly you, don't you remember? The insurance company first, the insurance agent second, and **you last**. Do you want to see an insurance agent squirm who is trying to sell you an annuity? Ask them about no surrender charge and no commission annuities. Knowledge is power for American Patriots.

Well, I forgot to mention annuities in qualified accounts like Roth IRAs or Traditional IRAs. Both of those are already tax-deferred, so you are putting a tax-deferred annuity inside a tax-deferred account. There is no need for that. With a recent enactment of ERISA's "Improving Investment Advice for Workers and Retirees," I suspect that insurance agents will not be selling you an annuity for your IRA or Roth IRA. There is too much fiduciary liability now. They will stick with the non-qualified (taxable) annuity sales only more than likely. More on this new ERISA rule a little later.

From a diversified portfolio perspective, annuities are essentially classified as fixed income. Therefore, if you wanted to invest in a variable annuity, put it in the **long-term bond** category. Remember your upper and lower limits. The insurance agent has an incentive to get you to put everything you own in an annuity. Why? Because they get paid 6.5% in commissions! Never forget that, by the way. Successful insurance agents are sly rascals who live high on the hog. You would be living high on the hog, too, if you sold a $100,000 annuity and made $6,500 for saying, "Sign here."

Think of yourself as Joe Biden with a stack of executive orders in front of you when you are talking to an insurance agent. There is a White House "insurance agent" telling poor old Joe to "sign here" and further tells him not to worry about what those executive orders say. Like they tell Joe Biden what to do and not to worry, your insurance agent will tell you the same thing. "Do not worry. Sign here."

CHAPTER TWENTY-TWO

Real Estate

You can certainly make money in real estate. I want to discuss investing in real estate ETFs, mutual funds, plus real estate investment trusts or REITs. If you are looking at putting your dollars to work in investment real estate, the you need to read another book. I have had a real estate license since 2006, but I use it primarily to advise clients on real estate transactions. I refer real estate *sales* to other more qualified real estate brokers. I do not want to go into all the nuances of buying and selling investment properties in this book. There are other authors way more qualified than me on that subject. My focus here is how to use real estate ETFs, mutual funds, and REITs within a portfolio design framework.

Investing in real estate within a diversified portfolio framework, you have four main choices. One is to invest in a real estate ETF. Another is to invest in a real estate mutual fund. Another is to invest directly in publicly-traded REITs that trade on the stock exchanges, and the final way to invest in real estate is via non-publicly traded REITs. However, these non-publicly traded REITs (sometimes disguised as Business Development Companies or BDCs) are places where your money goes to die. Let me start with these first because these have the most danger to your chance at growing your money. Non-publicly traded REITs (BDCs) are sold to investors typically by registered representatives at major and independent Wall Street firms. Why do they sell these? Simply because they pay outsized commissions. These non-publicly traded REITs are built like your typical Ponzi scheme. They take your money (principal) and turn it around and give a portion of it back to you as a dividend. For example, if you give them $100,000, they will invest it in commercial real estate like strip malls, regular malls, office buildings, and real estate under construction. A portfolio of this type of real estate will pay income from its leases. However, these non-publicly traded REITs will pay more than that to attract money from you. Perhaps you have seen an ad on television where they say they "are offering *10% monthly distribution and up to *21% targeted total returns." This is a non-publicly traded REIT, and this how they sell them to you. They do not tell you that that 10% monthly distribution is your principal's return. The 21% targeted total return is hocus-pocus. They have no clue if they will ever achieve that. They do not even care. All they care about is getting you to invest in their non-publicly traded REIT because once they have your money, then you are in trouble.

A typical non-publicly traded REIT may have a portfolio with a dividend rate of 4%. Still, they take some from everyone's principal, like another 4%, and pay (in the early years) a total of 8% to investors who are fools enough to invest in these. If you understand math correctly, this means that this investment is guaranteed to lose 4% each year. Except for the fact that you have to pay the people "managing" the non-publicly traded REIT or BDC. The people selling you this "investment" hire external commercial real estate managers that charge high fees. These external managers are not looking out for shareholders. They are looking out for themselves and their fees. This is called a conflict of interest, by the way. Typical manager fees can be 2% per year. Now, we are losing 6% per year on this "investment." Do not forget that they are finishing building out something with your money, either. They may have to obtain a loan, too. How does that not impact the return of your principal? Loans have costs. A lot of times, one non-publicly traded REIT "sells itself" to another non-publicly traded REIT managed by the same group of people. They call this a **roll-up,** and typically, it means that your 10 — 12 years for a return of principal is now going to take longer. How do you like these "investments" so far?

Other issues with these non-publicly traded REITs are their lack of liquidity and incorrect share value pricing. The management prices their share value, but not to worry. These people are entirely trustworthy. Ha! You see, when you buy one of these, then you have to keep it 10 — 12 years before you can get your principal back. Sorry, I meant to get some of your principal back. The odds of you having a long-term capital gain on this investment is slim-to-none. Let me ask you a question or two? How are inside shopping malls doing these days with the pandemic? How about office building leases? At my wife's company, their 80 person staff members are all working from home now, and her company just ended their office lease. They did not renew it, in order words. Now imagine how much rent they were paying for the whole floor of a Class A office building for 80 people. This is happening and will continue to happen for a while in this country until we overcome the pandemic. Tell me why you want to invest in a non-liquid investment that you are stuck in for 10 — 12 years, an investment that you cannot figure out what it is worth on any given day, and an investment that is full of real estate that is bailing out on landlords left and right. I will be here waiting on your answer. Meanwhile, I will move on for the people who are smart enough not to set their money on fire by investing in this garbage.

Now that I got that out of the way, we can move on to real estate ETFs and mutual funds. I will "circle back" to **publicly traded** REITs in a bit. If you look inside a popular real estate ETF, then you will notice that it holds things a lot different from those crappy non-publicly traded REITs. The real estate ETF will contain stuff like industrial warehouses (Amazon), cell phone towers, data centers (cloud computing), self-storage (U-Haul), apartments, and health care locations (assisted living/nursing homes). It will also hold a little bit of office, malls, and hotels (less than 15%). If you look inside a real estate mutual fund, you will see a very similar group of holdings. You may be asking whether a real estate ETF or a real estate mutual fund is the better choice? If you are comparing solely on fees and taxes, then the ETF will beat the mutual fund all day long, plus you can trade it throughout the day, whereas you cannot with a mutual fund. Of course, you want to look at the dividend yield, too, along with the managers' performance running the ETF or mutual fund compared to others. As you can imagine, commercial real estate did not do so well because of the pandemic. Residential real estate has done well during the pandemic, so should you invest in a residential real estate ETF or mutual fund? **NO!** If you did, you would not be diversifying your real estate dollars. Stick with broad-based real estate ETFs and mutual funds that are not overly concentrated in areas likely to underperform. Look inside them to see what is in their portfolio. The track record of a real estate mutual fund management team is essential. A management team that has been through periods where real estate has performed poorly, but they held up better is what you want. See how they did in bad periods, then you will understand their risk better.

You may be wondering. Why should you invest in a non-publicly traded REIT or BDC when you can buy several through the stock market? That's a good question. There is no need to buy a non-publicly traded REIT or BDC when you can buy a REIT on the stock exchanges. Again, this is another area where you have to do your homework. Real estate ETFs and mutual funds will be broader-based or diversified. Whereas publicly traded REITs are likely to be more focused. This is not in any way, shape, or form a recommendation, but Vornado Realty Trust has been around a long time. See their website for more information. https://www.vno.com/. Their REIT portfolio is focused on highly concentrated positions in two sectors of real estate. One is urban offices in New York City, and the other is retail in Manhattan. The rest of their portfolio consists of residential buildings and new developments, primarily in the New York City area. You can make money sometimes by investing in beaten-down sectors, and New York City right now may be an example. There are many stories of people fleeing New York City for no state income tax states. Houses in my county are being bought within a few hours because of the New Yorkers fleeing to Florida. People are fleeing to South Florida more than North Florida. However, we still have our share of new buyers in North Florida. One of my clients said they put in an offer of $5,000 over list price, and they did not get it. Not only did they not get it, but they said that house sold within three hours. Hedge funds are buying homes in Florida to resell them for a profit. Three houses in my neighborhood sold within three days this week. All three of them!

Perhaps, a REIT like the Vornado Realty Trust is something that you may want to research and consider for a portion of your diversified or focused portfolio. New York City real estate will rebound. It always does. The question is, how long will it take? Whether you should invest in a focused REIT like the Vornado Realty Trust or just invest in a diversified real estate ETF or mutual fund is your decision. You can find apartment REITs, health care REITs, public storage REITs, and a host of other concentrated or focused REITs that are publicly traded. If you are a risk-taker, then an exchange-listed (**publicly traded**) REIT may be for you if you are looking to build more of a focused portfolio. If you are more moderate or conservative, then a real estate ETF or mutual fund would be more appropriate for your diversified portfolio. Keep in mind that you will have upper and lower limits on how much to invest in your real estate asset class. You are not trying to solve the complexity of a black hole in space here. You are simply trying to figure out what type of real estate investment, (ETF, mutual fund, or REIT) and what percentage you should allocate with your investing dollars towards your diversified or focused portfolio. It is not that hard. Decide and revisit down the road.

CHAPTER TWENTY-THREE

Commodities

Most commodities are based on Energy, Agriculture, Precious, and Industrial Metals. Inside each of those categories, there are additional choices. For example, under Energy, you have WTI Crude Oil, Brent Crude, RBOB Gasoline, Natural Gas, and Heating Oil. Big oil producers like Chevron and Exxon Mobil will hedge their portfolios with commodities. Airlines will hedge their gas purchases for the fuel they need in the future with commodities. Natural gas producers will hedge the price of natural gas against the future price of natural gas. Farmers will hedge their crop prices with commodities. On the other side of the equation are the speculators or futures investors who place bets on the price of commodities. Some are successful, but the majority of them are not.

I did not mention anything about individual investors who invest in commodities if you noticed. However, there are ETFs and mutual funds that invest in commodities. A commodities allocation can be a good correlation offset against stocks, but I would not put a high percentage in this area.

There are things to watch out for with commodities ETFs and mutual funds. There are hidden risks like contango and backwardation. If you want to know more, then visit this site: https://www.investopedia.com/articles/07/contango_backwardation.asp. You have lost your marbles if you think I am going to explain the difference between contango and backwardation. Another risk is that these commodities funds are ETNs, in most cases. You may recall that ETNs based on commodities do not hold the stocks. They have **futures contracts** with maturity dates and payout at maturity inside the ETN, which is hopefully returned to the investor at some point. I will repeat it. There is issuer risk with ETNs, plus the commodities risk to go along with it—a double whammy of trouble, in other words.

Commodities ETFs will not correlate with the stocks in your diversified or focused portfolio. If you are trying to get a more broadly diversified portfolio, then perhaps a small portion of your investing dollars could be allocated towards commodities. I am not big fan of investing in commodities. The returns are not there over a longer term time period, in my opinion. Do some research on commodities returns and see for yourself.

CHAPTER TWENTY-FOUR

Natural Resources

Some ETFs drill down to specific sectors like oil, natural gas, lumber or timber, water, gold, silver, platinum, and agriculture. Some ETNs do the same. I would opt for the ETFs instead of the ETNs because you would own the stocks instead of futures on the stocks. For your diversified portfolio, I would probably limit your allocation to between 5% and 10% depending on your risk level. You can invest in natural resource ETFs and mutual funds instead of drilling down to sub-sectors like water, timber, or platinum. Did you even know that you could invest in water or timber? That's what I thought!

You are better off letting the experts do it and find an excellent natural resources ETF or mutual fund that is broad-based and spreads the risk among many sub-sectors. It is up to you whether you want to add this to your <u>diversified</u> portfolio or not. Remember, lumber prices have skyrocketed recently and the odds of that reversing are pretty good once the demand subsides. Therefore, putting on your critical thinking hat, you would realize that if you invest in timber now, you would be buying at a high.

Suppose you are looking to allocate dollars for a more <u>focused</u> portfolio and have an asset class that does not correlate with stocks. In that case, you may want to drill down to the sub-sectors in the natural resources space like gold, silver, platinum, water, timber, or other sub-sectors.

Natural resources have historically been shown to be an excellent correlation offset to stock asset classes. If that is your goal, then now you know.

CHAPTER TWENTY-FIVE

ESG

Environmental, Social, and Governance is what the acronym ESG means. This is a rapidly growing area of investment opportunity in the ETF and mutual fund space. In 2011, there were 99 ETFs and mutual funds in the sustainable landscape. At the end of 2020, there are now 392, according to Morningstar®. Many people want to invest with ETF or mutual fund firms that screen for sustainable companies or have good records.

People like electric cars. Of course, we can see that with our own eyes with companies like Tesla who has developed an entire business based on electric vehicles. Other car manufacturers like Audi, Ford, GM, Hyundai, Kia, Lamborghini, Mercedes, Porsche, Toyota and Volkswagen, and others have announced significant electric vehicle spending. This is a growth area without a doubt, but I would look more at the companies that supply the new technology to the auto manufacturers.

Of course, there are energy alternatives now like solar and wind. I expect more refinement in the clean energy area going forward. They still have a few kinks to work out, but this is America, and our technological leadership is unrivaled. I believe in good things to come in this area. However, the thing to keep in mind is that solar and wind are only a partial energy supply. It is not the be-all and end-all like liberals and progressives would have you believe. You still need backup power from utility companies, whether coal-fired plants or nuclear energy. Further, solar, for example, tends to work best in the part of the country that has a lot of sun. Duh! It does not work so well in states with harsh winters because the number of sunny days is less than favorable.

Environmental is an easy one. The tough ones are Social and Governance. Are they investing in social causes? Well, not exactly. It is more about investing in companies that are run well. They may have a diversified workforce with ample opportunities for all. Of course, most large companies are already doing the right thing by having a diverse workforce. Just because fake news tells you differently does not mean it is true. Not much of what they tell you is true, in my opinion. When it comes to the Social aspect of ESG, like anything else in life, there is always room for improvement.

My question for liberals and progressives is this:

> "What exact percentages should each company in America have as far as Asians, Blacks, Mixed Races, Native Americans, and Whites?"

The U.S. Census counts Hispanics with White people. Did you know that? Back to my question. After my liberal and progressive friends are completely stumped about the exact percentages and start insulting me, I usually follow that up with this question.

> "How many straight, gay, lesbian, or transgender people should each company hire, and in what percentages?"

Of course, they have no answer because they only use their head for a hat rack and repeat what they see on fake news television. Critical thinking does not happen with liberals and progressives. They are good at making accusations and making videos and screaming into their phones. In the last few weeks, they have suddenly rallied around the Asian-American Pacific Islander (AAPI) community. Before a few weeks ago, have you even heard of the AAPI? The liberals and progressives claim there is an outbreak of hate crimes. The facts are that there were 122 (in 2020) considered hate crimes by the Bureau of Justice Statistics. I would not think 122 to be a number that would cause me to believe this to be a significant problem in America. I do not like hate crimes, of course against anyone, but only 122 out of over 20,000,000 Asian people in America today. The prior year it was 49. This is what liberals and progressives do with numbers like this. They say, "Hate crimes against Asian Americans have more than doubled!" When in reality, there are more hate crimes against **white people** than any other group by far. See this website: https://www.justice.gov/hatecrimes/hate-crime-statistics for proof. This sudden announcement by the PINO that there is a rash of hate crimes against Asian Americans is only another attempt by liberals and progressives to **keep us divided**. This is their primary goal. If we are divided, we can never be united against them and their failed ideology.

Realize this. Most companies are good, donate to their local communities, or support causes they favor and are taking great strides to improve their hiring and training practices. It would help out a lot if the teachers' unions quit filling our kids with their failed ideology. As Rush Limbaugh liked to say, young people have "skulls full of mush" because of what liberals and progressives teach them. No company wants to hire some lunatic liberal or progressive who is like the crazy cat lady, otherwise known as "Karen," and makes screaming videos into her phone all day. How about the "Karen" that screams at you in a grocery store because you either are not wearing a mask or are wearing it wrong? If you are a business, you do not want to hire people like this? They are more trouble than they are worth if you ask me. Do not even try to convince "Karen" of anything. She will have none of it. You would be wasting your time. Leave her to her misery.

The governance part of ESG is where stockholders are given accurate and transparent information about their company, including all conflicts of interest. Further, it means that the board members and C-suite executives are not unduly influenced by political ideology and the political contributions to politicians. Companies in Silicon Valley do the opposite. They line the pockets of people in the swamp, so they can get away with whatever they want. Check out this website on Silicon Valley donations in the 2020 election. https://observer.com/2020/11/big-tech-2020-presidential-election-donation-breakdown-ranking/. Look at how much went to Democrats and Joe Biden in percentage terms. Now, you can see why we American Patriots have a problem.

Blue Anon is out to ruin everything. Liberals and progressives hate being labeled **Blue Anon,** by the way. It makes them go crazy. It would be nice if companies quit giving money to politicians, then they would have to ask regular folks for donations. After that, then perhaps they might actually do some work for the American people. This is not likely to ever happen, but it would be my idea of Utopia. We have something to strive for anyway. *Citizens United v. Federal Elections Commission* is the Supreme Court case decided in 2010 that allowed corporations, non-profits, labor unions, and associations to give as much as they want to politicians and political parties. President Obama was against this because he said that this decision

> "...gives the special interests and their lobbyists even more power in Washington."

How prophetic were those words? This is precisely what has happened. Think about the untouchable Silicon Valley tech firms who donate millions to the swamp and crooked Attorney Generals, Governors and Secretary of States. President Obama was spot on about this issue. There needs to be limits by big corporate donors because <u>the American people do not have any power over the politicians anymore</u>. Do you think a politician will listen to you, a $100 campaign donor, instead of a Silicon Valley tech firm that donates $1,000,000 to their campaign? Do you see the problem? We need to fix this somehow, someway. Somebody needs to file a lawsuit on behalf of the American people. Our political influence has been greatly diminished due to *Citizens United v. Federal Elections Commission*. As long as this law is in place, American Patriots have to keep fighting to overturn it.

Back to ESG. Some examples of poor ESG have happened in the past with oil or chemical spills, water plant problems, emissions scandals, and out and out bribery by corporate officials. Therefore, it is a good thing to screen for good corporate stewards. Morningstar's Research has ESG ratings now because of the growth in this area. They do the homework for you.

When building your diversified portfolio with ETFs or mutual funds, rest assured that you can find plenty of ESG fund choices to choose from to fill in your asset class blanks.

CHAPTER TWENTY-SIX

Cryptocurrencies

Cryptocurrencies are relatively new from their status as a form of currency. An analogy is to understand what is at stake with cryptocurrencies. It just so happens the recent 2020 US election is the perfect analogy. So how in the world is this analogy related to cryptocurrencies? What is the overriding issue of why the people in Washington, DC, wanted Trump gone? Money and power. If they rule our country, they control both: **money and power.**

Cryptocurrency fans, I believe, are being a little naive. The whole idea behind cryptocurrencies is to have a form of currency that <u>is not</u> regulated or controlled by any government. That is the primary appeal of cryptocurrencies. Now, let me ask you this question.

> "Do you believe that the same people who took out Donald Trump are going to let you have cryptocurrencies that they do not control, tax, or make money from?"

Look at your 2020 1040 form. The language about "virtual currencies" is on the 1040 form right now! Cryptocurrencies are taxed and regulated by the IRS today based on your holding period. These central bankers will figure out a way to gain control of cryptocurrencies. Wall Street firms will use their power and influence to gain control. How they will do it is that the world's central banks will outlaw Bitcoin and all the other cryptocurrencies and <u>create new cryptocurrencies</u> regulated and taxed and, more importantly, that they can control. A recent statement by the new SEC Commissioner Gary Gensler is very telling.

> "We will be working with Congress, and if they see fit, to try to bring some **protection** for people that want to invest in this speculative assets class."

SEC Commission Gensler is calling it protection, but I call it control. The other cryptocurrencies will drop like a hot rock once they develop a Congressionally approved cryptocurrency. If you think critically alongside me, you will realize that they will figure out a way to track your cryptocurrencies. I suspect that any time that a bank sees money leave their bank and go to a firm who trades in crypto, they will have to report it to the IRS in the same manner that they report cash transactions today. These people in Washington, DC, and the major credit card processing firms and Wall Street banks control the money now. They know every time that you move money from one place to another. Do not kid yourself. The government exists to control your life, tax your earnings and reward the people that help them win elections. It is all about the money. If you are stupid, then you will assume that there will not be any control by a government over cryptocurrencies. Good luck with that. Do you not believe me? Take a look at this link from the IRS website: https://www.irs.gov/newsroom/irs-has-begun-sending-letters-to-virtual-currency-owners-advising-them-to-pay-back-taxes-file-amended-returns-part-of-agencys-larger-efforts. Stop and read it. It is only five pages.

Now that you have read those pages and possibly others, maybe you will realize that the IRS will continue aggressive enforcement in this area. The new Treasury Secretary Janet Yellen made several remarks about cryptocurrencies recently at her confirmation hearing. In this article, you will notice statements along the lines of "they are not regulated, we should curtail their use, financial regulatory concerns, etc.," which is precisely what I said about cryptocurrencies. https://www.msn.com/en-us/money/markets/janet-yellen-suggests-curtailing-cryptocurrencies-such-as-bitcoin-saying-they-are-mainly-used-for-illegal-financing/ar-BB1cVd1R.

If you hide the fact that you invested in cryptocurrencies from the IRS, then you are evading taxes which is criminal. Therefore, if you invest in cryptocurrencies, please comply with the law and report gains and losses required by the IRS.

With cryptocurrencies, there are a few different ones that are most popular: Bitcoin ($58,871.86), Ethereum ($1,843.53), Litecoin ($196.63), and Bitcoin Cash ($530.27). Those are the prices from March 30th, 2021, and they fluctuate wildly from there, and I do mean wildly. On May 20, 2021, the prices were $41,770.00 for Bitcoin, $2,913.95 for Ethereum, $220.68 for Litecoin and $846.17 for Bitcoin Cash. How do you think they will fluctuate once the US Treasury Department, IRS, and Congress get fully involved? The swamp is on top of this right now as we speak. As Rush Limbaugh used to say, "Do not doubt me."

Buying cryptocurrencies has transaction fees depending on where you purchase your crypto and whether you use PayPal, Debit, Credit or ACH. Check out this article by the CEO of Visa about cryptocurrencies. https://www.coindesk.com/visa-may-add-cryptocurrencies-to-its-payments-network-says-ceo.

There are only 21 million Bitcoins, and supposedly, there will never be more than 21 million Bitcoins. Thus, the scarcity of it is also an attraction. There are multitudes of Bitcoin rivals. There are thousands worldwide. Did you know there are thousands of digital (virtual) currencies? That is what I thought!

Bitcoin makes up 60% of the cryptocurrency market, according to https://www.Coinbase.com. I do not think Bitcoin and the other popular cryptocurrencies are going away. If they want to play, they will have to play by Washington, DC's rules. However, I do not see how this will happen since there is no government control over virtual currencies today. I know that if you transfer $50,000 from your brokerage account to a Bitcoin account, then the IRS is going to know about it, and your bank is going to know about it. Do you believe that a bank will let you take money out of their bank and not charge you a fee for moving it to a virtual currency? They charge you if you move brokerage accounts right now. Of course, the bank's very own virtual currency will not charge a fee. Do you see how easy it is to gain control? The IRS will tax you going in and going out. As a matter of fact, the Treasury Department (IRS) announced that they want to know when there are any transactions in virtual currencies (cryptocurrencies) over $10,000. Here is an article on it. https://news.bitcoin.com/us-treasury-biden-tax-cryptocurrency-transfers-over-10000-reported-to-irs/

By the way, China recently announced its proprietary digital currency. Do you think the US, Russia and the United Kingdom, and other European countries are just going to sit idly by and not create their own digital currency? I do not think so. They will end up in control of cryptocurrencies, or at least the ones that matter — their own. Wow! Will you look at this. Hot off the press! The Federal Reserve just announced that they are looking at developing their own digital currency. https://www.cnbc.com/2021/05/20/the-fed-this-summer-will-take-another-step-ahead-in-developing-a-digital-currency.html?utm_content=Main&utm_medium=Social&utm_source=[1]

As with anything else in your diversified portfolio, you would categorize this into an asset class. In this case, it would be cash and cash equivalents. Then you would assign a percentage upper and lower limit. If you only commit 5% or 10% to Bitcoin, or Ethereum, then the worst that could happen is that you lose 5 — 10%. I do not recommend making a focused portfolio out of cryptocurrencies unless you keep the

1. https://www.cnbc.com/2021/05/20/the-fed-this-summer-will-take-another-step-ahead-in-developing-a-digital-currency.html?utm_content=Main&utm_medium=Social&utm_source=Twitter#Echobox_43ec3e5dee6e706af7766fffea512721_1621533836

percentage low compared to your overall net worth. You will need to stay on top of cryptocurrencies and read everything you can get your hands on because I suspect this to be an evolving asset class with many regulatory changes. Cryptocurrency is not a set it and forget type of investment.

CHAPTER TWENTY-SEVEN

Circle Back to Stocks

Now let us "circle back" to stocks and review what we have accomplished. We learned how to research and build a stock portfolio considering the eleven different sectors in the S&P 500®. We figured out how to distinguish between a diversified stock portfolio and a focused stock portfolio and how we should always open separate accounts for each type of stock portfolio. Opening different accounts allows us to evaluate both the diversified and focused stock portfolios. Our allocation to stocks can be split between a diversified and a focused portfolio based on the level of risk that we want in our stock portfolio.

Further, we learned that there are eleven main sectors in the S&P 500®. In building our diversified stock portfolio, we want to pick and research stocks in multiples of eleven to have broad exposure to the stock market. If we're going to be a little more aggressive, then perhaps we would add a focused stock portfolio for 22% to 33% of our funds available for investing. We should remember to put the focused stocks in a separate account from our diversified portfolio account to see the performance of each stock portfolio over time.

When we build a diversified stock portfolio invested across eleven sectors, we realize that we will have winners and losers. Our expectation for the performance of our diversified stock portfolio will probably perform similarly to that of the S&P 500® index. We know this going in, and we are okay with this fact.

When we build a focused stock portfolio, on the other hand, then we realize that this is the **Explore** portion of our overall investment portfolio. Our opportunity to exceed the performance of a diversified stock portfolio is to add a focused stock portfolio concentrated in a limited number of stocks and put in a separate account on its own.

Finally, when it comes to stock investing and evaluating our positions a year later, we will compare the stock we chose with the stock sector. If the sector is also performing poorly, **it could be the sector** and not the stock. However, if the sector is doing well and the stock is not doing well, then we have a reason to evaluate selling it. This is very important. We must compare our stock's performance with the sector's performance. When we make this comparison, we will know whether we need to sell it.

CHAPTER TWENTY-EIGHT

Circle Back to ETFs

When we "circle back" to ETFs, we know that ETFs stands for Exchange Traded Funds. Further, we learned to stay far away from ETNs, or Exchange Traded **Notes** because we would rather own stocks in an ETF than futures in an ETN. ETNs have issuer risk, and several ETNs have had significant losses, primarily revolving around leveraged and inverse ETNs.

The taxation of ETFs is what separates them from other investments, especially mutual funds. ETFs have a creation and redemption process that makes them appealing to individual investors. ETFs trade like a stock and have their own cost basis. As the investor in an ETF, you are not subject to the whims of other panicky investors like in mutual funds. As an ETF investor, you realize that your ETF positions are tax-deferred in a taxable account until sold.

The beauty of ETFs is the fact that you can build a diversified ETF portfolio based on a 100% Core (Blend) strategy by investing in index-based ETFs. We realize that if we invest in index-based ETFs, our performance will match the ETF index (minus small management fees). Therefore, we can never do worse than the index. If we choose actively managed ETFs, we risk underperforming the index or asset class category. Conversely, we could out-perform the index with actively managed ETFs. It all depends on our risk level whether to go 100% indexed-based ETFs or mix in actively managed ETFs for a chance at out-performance.

We can have a diversified ETF portfolio with a 100% Core index strategy if we are a moderate risk investor. If we are more growth-oriented or more aggressive in risk tolerance, we can choose a mix between **Core and Explore** for a percentage split based on that risk level. For example, we could have a 75% Core or diversified ETF portfolio and a 25% Explore or focused ETF portfolio. We know to adjust those percentages up or down based on the level of risk that is acceptable to us. In addition, we know to have two accounts to put the diversified ETF portfolio in one account and the focused ETF portfolio in another account to track our performance.

We know that asset classes included in the diversified ETF portfolio are large-cap, mid-cap, small-cap, developed markets, and emerging markets. We realize that we can use the index in each category or break them down into different sub-asset classes. For example, equal-weighting, fundamental indexing, or market-weighting in conjunction with the asset class chosen. We know that equal-weighting, fundamental indexing, and market-weighting ETFs are available in almost all asset classes.

For the focused ETF portfolio, we know that we simply add our focused bets with things like sector funds, such as consumer discretionary, technology, health care, industrials, materials, real estate, and the other sectors that make up our eleven sectors. If we want to get risker, we may consider other Explore investments. We know that it is crucial to read and research things like cryptocurrencies, hedge replication funds, managed futures, and or SPACs.

We know there is no bang for the buck investing in US government bonds or agencies ETFs on the fixed-income side of our diversified ETF portfolio. Nor is there much benefit to investing in municipal bonds ETFs. Further, we realize that investing in a bank loan or floating rate ETFs comes with many nasty surprises. Certificates of Deposit may be appropriate for a separate emergency fund but not in our diversified ETF portfolio. Preferred stocks ETFs are a fixed income class, as we learned, and come with a ton of risk due to their long maturities. Our principal can get crushed with a preferred stocks ETF. Commodities and natural resources may have a place in a focused ETF portfolio. Still, we know that commodities involve futures contracts, and even years of study will not get us up to speed on understanding how futures contracts work. Therefore, we should stay away from commodities altogether. Natural resources can sometimes be a place to put dollars in our ETF portfolio when we want to have asset classes that do not correlate with stock ETFs.

Currencies from other countries are essentially money market funds denominated in those other countries' currencies. We should not expect any outlandish out-performance if we invest in the Swedish krona,, for example. We will likely receive money market rates at best which are relatively paltry right now, and we may even lose money when the US dollar strengthens against those other currencies.

We learned how to establish our upper limits and lower limits for each ETF asset class. We realize that we probably want to keep our choices between 12 — 20 or so ETFs for a diversified ETF portfolio. It depends on if we're going to drill down in each asset class with things like Factors such as high beta, quality, momentum, or ESG, or different styles of market investing like equal-weighting, fundamental indexing, or stick with market-weighting.

By adding foreign bond and sovereign bond ETFs and mutual funds to our diversified portfolio, we may squeeze out a little more in dividends with added growth potential. Instead of building our fixed income portion of our diversified portfolio by understanding what is going on in Singapore, or South Korea, we rely on the ETF and mutual fund managers to do the legwork for us.

There are developed market corporate bonds, emerging market bonds denominated in US dollars, emerging market bonds in the local currency, and sovereign bonds issued by governments like Germany, France, Japan, and the United Kingdom. We fill up our fixed-income bucket or asset classes with these fixed-income choices or asset classes, all the while slanting our fixed-income exposure based on our level of risk.

CHAPTER TWENTY-NINE

Circle Back to Mutual Funds

Now we can "circle back" to mutual funds. Regarding mutual funds, we realize that sometimes we have to choose from a mutual fund selection because that may be our only choice inside of our 401(k) or another type of retirement plan. With that in mind, we can utilize what we already discussed regarding ETFs and incorporate it into our diversified or focused mutual fund portfolio. The thing we want to look at with mutual funds is whether or not there are index funds to choose from in our 401(k). Index funds will have the lowest mutual fund expenses compared to actively managed mutual funds. So, in looking at building our diversified or focused mutual fund portfolio, we want to try and find all the index funds available to us in our 401(k) or another type of retirement plan. Once we find those, we fit those into our asset classes mentioned previously (i.e., large-cap, mid-cap, small-cap, developed markets, etc.) After making the index fund choices, we move to the actively managed favorites to fill in the gaps in our diversified or focused mutual fund portfolio. When looking at the actively managed alternatives, you still want to look at low expense funds, plus management tenure, whether operated by a team of managers or a star manager. In addition, you want to see how the actively managed fund has performed over time and compare that to the index for that asset class. In other words, if there is no index mutual fund in the developed markets, then you want to choose a developed markets actively managed fund that has low expenses, good management, and has performed well against its index benchmark. You would do the same for each asset class that does not have an index fund offering in your 401(k) or another type of retirement plan.

By now, you should understand how to design your diversified mutual fund portfolio or focused mutual fund portfolio. You simply choose the core asset classes based on your level of risk, select your index funds, then sprinkle the actively managed funds available around the index funds. Sometimes, you will find your 401(k) or another type of retirement plan is limited, and they do not even have certain asset classes. In addition, you may find that there is only one choice in an asset class, and it is not an index fund. Of course, this means you have to adapt to the mutual fund menu of options you have. Do not fret over it. Just make your choices and then revisit in a year.

I wanted to throw variable annuities into the mix under mutual funds because technically, the choices in your variable annuity are mutual fund-like sub-accounts. Typically, you have an abundance of sub-accounts to choose from in a variable annuity, so building your diversified or focused sub-account portfolio will be easier than your 401(k) or another type of retirement plan. Some of these variable annuities may have 60 — 80 or more sub-accounts. Of course, we are assuming that you already own a variable annuity. You want to have it diversified adequately. If, after what I told you in this book about annuities in general and you still want to buy a variable annuity, see if you can buy one without commissions. There are registered investment advisers who can offer these **no commission variable annuities without any surrender charges**. That would be better than purchasing a variable annuity with a ten-year surrender charge that pays your insurance agent 6.5% or more for saying, "Sign here." Oh by the way, whenever there is a bonus attached to an annuity, then you can guarantee the insurance agent is getting more than 6.5% in commissions. Double digit commissions is what most insurance agents receive when they offer you a bonus annuity. Your surrender period may expand to as much as 15 years with bonus annuities.

CHAPTER THIRTY

Circle Back to Bad Investments

It is essential to understand this chapter. By "circling back" to the bad investments that are out there, we will refrain from making poor investment decisions that we will regret.

Annuities are sold by insurance agents who have the least experience and securities licensing required for designing investment portfolios. We realize that **we can keep our principal,** and we do not have to annuitize any annuity. We know never to annuitize our principal because it is lost forever once we do. Especially when you are about to retire and have a pension, always take the lump sum pension option! <u>Do not take the guaranteed option of your pension</u>! If you can get a lump sum, then take it. That way, you can control the income from it. If you do the opposite and take the guaranteed pension income, then your lump sum is gone forever.

There is no bang for the buck with fixed annuities or fixed indexed annuities. Their returns will mimic a fixed income-like return. We know this about fixed indexed annuities because they will average down to a fixed income-like return when you factor in the good years with the bad years. All those fancy charts that the insurance agent showed us where we are guaranteed never to lose money are simply not accurate. They do not tell you about lost opportunity costs. If we only make a fixed income like return in an annuity, then perhaps we could have done better than that in a diversified ETF portfolio with our mix of asset classes. We are very comfortable knowing that we can build our income stream with a diversified ETF portfolio and adjust our withdrawals up or down as needed. An annuity with "10% free withdrawals" is only a sales pitch. The reality is that we probably would never pull out 10% every year from our diversified ETF portfolio. Why would we want to pull out 10% per year from an annuity? It makes no sense unless you are trying to remove all your money from the annuity. If that is your goal, then there is a better way to remove all your money from an annuity. All you do is take a **five-year settlement option**. Then the annuity company will pay you back your entire annuity principal plus interest over five years with no surrender charges! This annuity withdrawal will have an exclusion ratio that we learned was a split of the principal and the earnings. However, we know that the return we made on the annuity is not likely to be much of anything. A five-year settlement option annuity will have a high principal interest earnings exclusion ratio. This method is the best way to get out of our annuity, no matter what kind of annuity, fixed, fixed-indexed, or variable annuity. Simply take a five-year settlement option if you want out **without surrender charges**. There are no surrender charges to do this. Accept the fact that we may have screwed up by buying the annuity in the first place, and we can get our money back spread out over the next five years and invest it in a diversified stock, ETF, or mutual fund portfolio.

You may be wondering about getting out of a variable annuity in your IRA or Roth IRA. What you do is set up an IRA or Roth IRA at your brokerage firm, then take a five-year settlement option from your variable annuity IRA or Roth IRA. Once per year, you can receive money from an IRA or Roth IRA and put it back into the IRA or Roth IRA brokerage account within 60 days. This way, even though you will receive a 1099-R for the five-year settlement option from the variable annuity IRA or Roth IRA, you will have the proof that you put it back into your brokerage IRA or Roth IRA within 60 days, thus saving taxes. The only caveat with this strategy is that you can only do this type of transaction once every 12 months, but this is not an issue with a five-year settlement as long as you request it once per year for five years. You have to make sure that you deposit it into your IRA or Roth IRA within 60 days once you receive one of those five-year settlement option payments. Otherwise, you will owe taxes on any portion that you do not re-deposit within those 60 days.

The bottom line on getting your money out of an annuity, whether from a non-qualified taxable annuity or a qualified annuity (IRA or Roth IRA), is the fact that you can utilize a five-year settlement option.

Another sales pitch from insurance agents is that this annuity is "tax-deferred." Excuse me. If you build a diversified ETF portfolio, it is also tax-deferred until you decide to sell something. These insurance agents are such fools for insurance company marketing sales pitches. They do not think critically. They are like liberals and progressives who have no critical thinking skills and believe everything they see on the fake news channels.

If you are doing things correctly and building your diversified ETF portfolio for the long term, then you will not be jumping in and out of ETFs, nor would you with an annuity. Further, if you decide to make a change or withdraw from a diversified ETF portfolio, you can control the taxes. Some withdrawals may receive lower capital gains treatment. Whereas in the non-qualified annuity, it is all LIFO ordinary income to cost basis. In the diversified ETF portfolio, you may be able to make a withdrawal and eliminate or reduce any taxes on it by selling losers against winners. <u>You have no control with the annuity</u>. I know I am repetitive, but annuities are taxed with ordinary income until you reach your cost basis. It is crucial to think critically about your decision to buy an annuity (before you do it) or whether you would be better off controlling your tax liabilities with a diversified ETF portfolio. **Control is always better**, regardless of what insurance agents try and convince you.

Today's hot thing is insurance agents are selling indexed universal <u>life insurance</u> and saying it is better than a diversified or focused portfolio. If that is true, why are several insurance companies being sued for selling indexed universal life policies? Because insurance agents sell them the same way, they sell annuities. They tell you about "tax-deferral and tax-free withdrawals" while failing to properly advise you about the **impact of loans** on a life insurance policy. Some of these insurance agents promote "private banking" by utilizing your indexed universal life policy. The problem with indexed universal life is that the interest rate assumptions shown by your insurance agent **will never happen**. Everything they offer you will crash like a house of cards once you start those "tax-free" loans. If you need life insurance, then, by all means, buy life insurance. I am a big believer in having enough life insurance to protect your family. Your choices are term, universal life, and whole life. You cannot afford whole life, so stick with term or universal life, whether it is variable universal life or the more conservative indexed universal life. Whole life salespeople like to talk about paid-up additions and dividends. Neither of those items takes away from the fact that whole life is the most expensive type of permanent life insurance you can buy. You can buy twice as much in death benefit with universal life compared to whole life. Do not fall for the "tax-free income" from life insurance sales pitch. "Tax-free income" involves loans, and the loans never work out as presented in those fancy presentations and illustrations.

Sometimes, you may run into a real smart-aleck insurance agent who thinks what I am telling you is wrong. If so, then ask Mr. Brilliance if he will run a life insurance illustration for you at **guaranteed rates and ask him to illustrate all that "tax-free" income involving loans at guaranteed rates, too**. In other words, run the illustration at guaranteed interest assumptions and guaranteed loan assumptions. He will likely need to change his pants after asking him to do that guaranteed illustration. Mr. Brilliance will likely not produce such an illustration because it will kill his sale to you. The last thing Mr. Brilliance wants to do is kill his sale. Trust me. (P.S. You do not have to tell him where you learned about guaranteed assumptions.) Those tax-free loans implode when you run the insurance illustration at guaranteed rates (not current assumptions).

I personally do not know of any professional women selling these plans. Most professional women that I know are way too smart to sell a "tax-free income" indexed life plan with loans that blow up in the end. Remember, insurance agents want to get your money. They do not care what happens afterwards, because they received the commission already. Men are hunters. It is all about the hunt.

RegD or private placements are structured precisely like Ponzi schemes. That is a true statement. They pay you initially with your principal. We are not that stupid and realize that we could do the same thing with our own money. Why the heck do we want to invest in something for 10 — 12 years and then find out that we got "rolled up" for another handful of years before we even have a shot at getting our principal back? This area is the most significant area for Ponzi schemes. If we invest in a RegD or private placement, then we would be more than likely setting our money on fire.

Any investment manager with more than $100,000,000 under management has to file Form 13-F with the US Securities and Exchange Commission. This Form 13-F is essentially a list of their discretionary holdings. Hedge replication funds are ETFs or mutual funds that build their hedge replication from these publicly available Form 13-F filings. This is how they do it. What does this tell us? It should be understood that hedge replication ETFs and mutual funds are investing based on a hedge fund's prior quarter's holdings. Therefore, it stands to reason that hedge funds may alter their positions at the end of the calendar quarter to keep their strategies from guess who? You and hedge replication funds. The SEC Form 13-F is required within 45 days of the end of a calendar quarter, so a hedge replication fund is 45 days late on changing its portfolios. The funny thing is that we now realize that we can do the same thing as the hedge replication funds do because all Form 13-F filings are publicly available via the

SEC's EDGAR database. We know we can find EDGAR here: https://www.sec.gov/edgar/searchedgar/companysearch.html and do our hedge fund research. We can follow a hedge fund's strategy for our focused portfolio. You may even find that hedge funds invest in ETFs. Wouldn't that be a surprise?

One of the worst investments that we can ever make, besides private placements (i.e., Ponzi schemes), are **non-publicly** traded REITs or Business Development Companies (BDCs). We are not stupid. We now know that if we want to add real estate as one of our asset classes, we choose between publicly traded REITs (i.e., Vornado Realty Trust), real estate ETFs, and real estate mutual funds. Further, we realize that if we want to have a focused real estate asset class, we can drill down to specific REITs like apartment REITs, public storage REITs, cell tower REITs, and others. There is simply no good reason to ever invest in a non-publicly traded REIT because we know it is a black hole where our money goes to die.

Cryptocurrencies are all the rage right now, but research is scarce on cryptocurrencies. Plus, who do you trust with your money? We know that if we decide to invest in crypto, we need to do a ton of reading and research because there are thousands of different virtual currencies out there, and there will likely be thousands more. In addition, we will only invest in cryptocurrencies as part of an asset class in our diversified or focused portfolio and put a percentage limit on it. Also, we realize that the IRS is already inquiring on Form 1040 about any virtual currency (i.e., cryptocurrencies) transactions and holdings. I am confident they will treat it as either a short-term capital gain or loss (ordinary income or loss) or a long-term capital gain or loss based on your holding period. Further, we fully understand the risk of government interventions, the tax authorities worldwide, and political influence by banks and Wall Street firms even if we disagree with the author's opinion. Finally, we will go in with our eyes wide open when investing in cryptocurrencies and limit our exposure.

CHAPTER THIRTY-ONE

Rebalancing Stock Portfolios

Once you have built your diversified or focused portfolio, you need to monitor it. Monitoring your portfolio is easy to do with most brokerage firms by utilizing alerts by email or text. These alerts will be based on the criteria that you set. Suppose you chose the 33-stock portfolio. To set up alerts for this 33-stock portfolio, you want to input an **up** percentage gain and a **down** percentage loss. In other words, you would set up an **up 3% alert** and at the same time a **down 3% alert** for each of the stocks in your 33-stock portfolio. These alerts are to "keep you in the game" by being aware of the movement of your 33 stocks. These 3% alerts are not meant to be sell points. They are only meant for you to evaluate your stocks.

After you have the 3% alerts in place, you need to decide how much of a worst-case decline you will accept. Are you okay with a 10% worse case decline, or are you more forgiving where you will allow yourself as much as a 15% or 20% decline before selling your stock position? You have to decide the percentage decline that you will accept. You need at least a 10% worse case decline because stocks move around a lot. If you only had a 5% worse case decline percentage, then you would be making sell trades all the time, and you would never get anywhere. Even a 10% worse case decline percentage may be too restrictive, but everyone is different. It all depends on your acceptable level of risk.

If you are investing in stocks, you have two things to do when a stock hits your downside percentage of 10%, 15%, or 20%. The first thing you do is evaluate the sector of your stock. The best way to do this is to look at a Sector Index ETF. SPDR® ETFs are some of the most popular sectors ETFs, and they have all eleven (11) sectors of the S&P 500®. Here is the link to their website: https://www.sectorspdr.com/sectorspdr/sectors. Click on the performance tab, and you will see the performance of each of the 11 sectors. Look for the sector that your stock is in and evaluate the recent performance. Is the sector also in a decline that matches your alert? If so, then this means that your stock **is not** the problem. Conversely, if the recent performance of your sector is holding up well, but your stock is not, then you have a reason to sell it.

My point for you in setting your alert percentages is to evaluate your stock once it hits your 10%, 15%, or 20% downside alert. The 3% alerts are just to keep you on your toes. There is nothing to do with 3% alerts. You want to be kept aware of the movement of your stock in the short term. Sometimes, you will see a 3% move in a day or two. Other times, it may take a week or two, and yet other times, it may take a month or two before you see a 3% move in your stock. Let's hope your 3% moves are always up.

Do not even try to skip this step because you would be investing willy-nilly. I do not like willy-nilly investing. It sets you up for inevitable failure.

CHAPTER THIRTY-TWO

Rebalancing Fund Portfolios

Rebalancing when it comes to your diversified or focused ETF or mutual fund portfolios is a little different from rebalancing individual stocks. With your ETF or mutual fund portfolio, you should already be investing in the index for each asset class. If you invest in the respective indexes, you already know that your performance will closely match the index. Therefore, you do not have to worry about under-performing your index on your main categories of asset classes like large-cap, mid-cap, small-cap, developed markets, and emerging markets. However, you may want to evaluate periodically when you drill down in those asset classes and choose equal-weighting, fundamental indexing, or market-weighting. Set your 3% alerts like with stocks as described earlier. The difference with your ETF and mutual fund alerts is to compare the differences between equal-weighting, fundamental indexing or, market-weighting. Why is this important? Because I want you to understand these differences. Once you let a year go by, you can see how each of these worked in your portfolio during that period. Next, you want to evaluate that one year. Was it a down year? Was it a mediocre year, or was it a good year? How did equal-weighting perform during that period? How did fundamental indexing perform during that period? How did market-weighting perform during that period? Do not make the mistake of just looking at past performance. That does not matter since it has nothing to do with the diversified portfolio or focused portfolio you designed. Do you follow me?

I already know the answer to those questions about investing styles, but there is nothing better than a real-world experience for you. Real-world experience will help you make good decisions on rebalancing your ETF or mutual fund portfolio. You are likely to find out that market-weighting does better when the market is going up strongly. Equal-weighting and fundamental indexing are going to do well during periods of **volatility**. If the stock market is jumping around a lot and especially in your asset class index, then the equal-weighting is going to hold up much better than a market-weighted index in the same asset class. Also, in a period where value stocks are doing better than growth stocks, then your fundamental indexing will do well because it is based on sound fundamentals of the underlying companies in the ETF or mutual fund. So, you want to be aware of whether we are in a growth period or a value period. If we are in a growth period, then ask yourself, are we in a volatile growth period or a more stable one (slow growth)?

Further, you need to look at each of the asset classes to evaluate them for these kinds of differences. Move from equal-weighting to market-weighting based on what you learn about market volatility. You may find that you are more comfortable with equal-weighting if you do not like a lot of volatility. On the other hand, you may find that you want fast-moving, high-flying stock markets, so you are okay with market-weighting. After the stock market has had a significant pullback, then perhaps fundamental indexing may be your best choice because those companies will have sound fundamentals and should do well going forward. Another alternative is to spread your asset class dollars in all three: equal-weighting, fundamental indexing and market-weighting.

You will have some actively managed ETFs or mutual funds in your portfolio due to limitations within your 401(k) or another type of retirement account. Therefore, you will evaluate against the index for that asset class in those instances. If you have other choices, you have a reason for moving the funds in that particular asset class if it is doing poorly.

I still want you to set alerts at your 3% up and down levels for each asset class. In addition, I want you to decide if your downside is 10%, 15%, or 20% for each of your ETFs or mutual funds in your diversified or focused portfolios. Let your ETFs and mutual funds go up because they will eventually have a pullback of 10%, 15%, or 20%. Therefore, your alerts will be in place automatically at higher levels. Do you see?

Within your **Explore** portion of your diversified or focused ETF or mutual fund portfolios, you may have more evaluating to do concerning alerts. For example, if you picked a REIT instead of a sector real estate ETF or mutual fund, you would need to set alerts to compare with the real estate asset class sector. You would repeat this process for other sectors where you are trying for out-performance with your Explore portion. Further, you may have a combination of a diversified ETF or mutual fund portfolio and have your Explore portion allocated to individual stocks. If so, you would follow the rebalancing described in the previous chapter on Rebalancing Stock Portfolios. Compare how your stock is doing with the sector that it is within.

By now, you should have a good idea after having read this far in my book whether you want to do things yourself or hire a professional **registered investment adviser**. If you are like Joe Biden and cannot do anything without a script written by your handlers, perhaps building your own diversified or focused portfolio is not for you. Poor old Joe Biden just had his first press conference, and he had a script with pictures of the press people and the answers to the questions that they were going to ask him. (Pre-scripted.) The way they are taking advantage of Joe Biden is sad and not fair to people with dementia. Let the poor guy enjoy time with his family while he still knows who the hell they are, for Pete's sake. By the way, "For Pete's sake day" is February 26th each year if you want to celebrate it. Every day is a holiday!

You can see that conservatives like me are compassionate people, unlike liberals and progressives. They hate everybody and claim to be the party of compassion. What a fallacy! If they were the party of compassion, there would be no accusations thrown at the people they oppose. There are countless murders in big Democratic (Blue Anon) cities every week, yet there is not a peep from them. Sadly, most of these occur in black communities. Why do black people continue to support Democratic candidates? They do nothing for the black community except keep them accountable to the government for handouts and putting their children in failing schools run by teachers' unions. A hand-up would be better. **Give all American people a good education**. Democrats are against that, as recently exposed by the teacher's unions across the country in Blue Anon states during the pandemic. Those Blue Anon teachers' unions got exposed! They will get away with it unless parents stand up to the Blue Anon teachers' unions and replace those sorry a** school board members.

You cannot get a good job if you drop out of high school. Duh! Educational opportunities exist in religious schools, charter schools, and prep schools. We need to figure out a way to get minority children to those types of schools to get the best education possible. Perhaps, this goal might be a good reason to run for your local school board. Making things better for minority communities has to start somewhere. That is probably the best place to start by taking back control of Blue Anon cities' failed education system.

We do not have a problem with schools in my county because our public schools are consistently ranked as the highest in Florida. We do not put up with any liberal and progressive crap where I live. We will throw you out of office if you try to implement any crazy liberal or progressive policies. That is the attitude you need to have in Blue Anon cities and states. Get busy.

CHAPTER THIRTY-THREE

Understanding Fiduciaries

I wanted to briefly describe the differences in fiduciaries because you must understand why you should use a **full-time fiduciary** and not a part-time fiduciary. The Department of Labor has implemented a new final rule that **favors investors** and requires that certain disclosures be made in writing. In addition, the fact that the disclosures are made in writing does not relieve your financial advisor or insurance agent from fiduciary liability. In other words, you as the investor are not signing away any of your rights by signing these ERISA disclosures. These new disclosure forms are based on the "Improving Investment Advice for Workers and Retirees" exemption. If you are crazy like me and like to read the fine print, then you can visit this site for more information. https://www.dol.gov/agencies/ebsa/about-ebsa/our-activities/resource-center/fact-sheets/improving-investment-advice-for-workers-and-retirees.

Essentially, here are the nuts and bolts of this ERISA final rule that was just implemented here in 2021. A financial advisor (or insurance agent) who asks you to roll over your 401(k) or another type of retirement plan to an IRA rollover account must disclose to you in writing the **specific reasons** they are recommending this transaction. In addition, they have to show you why it is in your best interest to initiate this transaction. They should do this by offering you **in writing** all the "extra services" that you will receive that you do not receive from your 401(k) or another type of retirement plan. This written disclosure also includes any time your financial advisor asks you to roll over or transfer an **IRA to an IRA** at their firm. It also consists of a

Roth 401(k) to a Roth IRA rollover or a Roth to a Roth. It includes a SEP-IRA to an IRA rollover and a SIMPLE IRA to an IRA rollover. The bottom line is that any time a financial advisor asks you to move an account, that is **any retirement plan or any type of IRA or Roth IRA,** they will need to provide the "specific reasons" and all the disclosures of their additional services offered. Finally, they will also need to compare the fees you are currently paying to the fees they will be charging you. In almost all cases, you will find the 401(k) fees are lower, but your investment adviser adds a whole plethora of services that you do not currently have with your 401(k).

I can tell you that there are already several insurance companies that will not allow their insurance licensed agents to sell any type of retirement account because of this ERISA final rule. They will only allow sales of non-qualified annuities, so they do not have to comply with this ERISA final rule. What does that tell you about insurance companies? It should tell you that they are in business for themselves and their agents and **not you**.

Other parts of this ERISA final rule mainly apply to record-keeping, compliance, and adherence for financial advisors that do not involve workers, retirees, or investors. They put some teeth into this ERISA final rule, too. If a financial advisor is audited by the EBSA and found not in compliance, they can be disqualified from doing any rollover transactions for ten (10) years! Yikes! Therefore, you can expect two things. You should see significant fee and services disclosures in writing when a financial advisor asks you to roll over your account to their firm, along with the specific reasons for doing so. (Financial advisors have to create these documents from scratch, so there will not be any uniformity in them.) My disclosures are on my website under "Disclosures" and ERISA Disclosures https://marianfs.com. These ERISA Disclosures were created by RIA Rules, LLC and are copyrighted.

On a side note, I own a company entitled RIA Rules, LLC specializing in complying with this new ERISA rule and other rules for small investment adviser firms regulated by states. You can find out more about this firm at https://riarules.com. If you are a small registered investment adviser, you may want to look at the RIA Rules, LLC website.

I suspect that you will see financial advisors lower their fees on all of their business clients. I cannot tell you how many big firms are out there who have been sailing along, gathering millions and billions in assets-under-management and charging fees of up to 2.5% and more. That does not count the investment expenses like the ETFs or mutual funds they choose. Oops! Therefore, several of these high fee firms will have to reach a business decision to figure out how to lower their fees. Otherwise, when they put in writing that their **all-in-fee** to investors like you is well over 3% per year, then you might decide <u>not to do business with a firm like that</u>. Hopefully, you will look for a more **reasonable** registered investment advisory firm to work with—one whose all-in fee is closer to 1.5%, including the ETF and mutual fund investments. A 1.5% all-in fee to a registered investment adviser is reasonable for the work they perform.

Notice, I did not say broker-dealer. Registered investment advisers **have always been fiduciaries,** whereas registered representatives have <u>never been fiduciaries</u>. Most of the time, registered representatives are known as dual registered. Dual registered means that they can sell you things like annuities, non-publicly traded REITs (BDCs), RegDs, promissory notes, unit investment trusts, and other things that make them money and not you. When these registered representatives think it is appropriate, then they will put on their "fiduciary hat" for one transaction when they have to put it on. They will be forced to wear that fiduciary hat more often now because of this ERISA final rule. As with most regulations, this one will benefit clients and law firms who go after the non-compliant actors.

I thought it was vital for you to understand the differences between someone (born male or female) who works solely at a registered investment adviser ***without*** a broker-dealer affiliation instead of someone like a registered representative who wears two hats. You never know what hat they are wearing. Stick with the registered investment adviser every time if you would rather enjoy your life than build diversified and focused portfolios. Hopefully, this book has demonstrated the expertise of registered investment advisers like me. I wrote this book from my professional experiences throughout my career. Besides researching some website links, the words in this book came mainly from my experiences over my 33-year career.

I wonder about this binary and non-binary thing. What will happen to Women's History Month if we are fools enough to go along with the non-binary definition of everyone? Liberals and progressives are people we usually would make fun of, but somehow, they managed to gain power in Washington, DC. We need to take it away from them with our "Make America Great Again" focus. President Donald Trump came up with that slogan, but that slogan is more significant than him alone. As the American people, we should never give up on the attainment of that goal. There is absolutely nothing wrong with wanting the best for America and its people. Never apologize for that focus. Our future depends on our success. We American Patriots need to take back control at every election going forward. As long as I live, I will not give up or give in. Neither should you.

CHAPTER THIRTY-FOUR

Elder Care

This chapter is a long one, but probably one of the most important chapters that you will ever read in your life. So, do not skip it. You need to know about everything in this chapter.

We all face it at one point or another in our lives. Parents who are blessed to live a long life need a lot of care and attention towards the end of their lives. People do not realize everything involved in caring for an aging parent, nor the aftermath after they pass away. Since I have dealt with this on numerous occasions in my career as a financial planner, I thought that I would offer you some pointers if you find yourself in this situation. In addition, I want to explain how you can plan and save your family members a lot of headaches.

Let's start with the Revocable Living Trust. A Revocable Living Trust is a document that accomplishes a lot of things. It provides for successor trustees in case you become incapacitated. It provides for beneficiaries after your death in the exact manner and percentages you choose. It eliminates the need to go to court, pay court costs and probate fees to an attorney, which can easily exceed 3% of your estate.

Further, it eliminates automatic delays concerning probate where things have to be published in the local paper and start a 60 - 90 waiting period for creditors to file any outstanding liens they may have against the estate. It allows a power of attorney to be named to pay the bills and other items. However, you want to be careful who you name as your power of attorney. They need to be someone trustworthy. The other issue with a power of attorney is that it has to be drafted correctly, or your financial institution may not accept it. You may be better off using the financial institution's power of attorney form rather than the one drafted by your attorney or an online prepared durable power of attorney. The reason is your durable power of attorney does not relieve your financial institution from someone using your power of attorney to their financial advantage. In comparison, the financial institution's power of attorney protects them against unscrupulous relatives. Since you signed and had notarized their financial institution form, they know you did it while competent because they saw you sitting in front of them when they notarized it.

Conversely, if your adult daughter suddenly pops into a bank branch and shows them a durable power of attorney document and wants access to all of your accounts, then how do they know it is real? How do they know that you are incompetent to handle your affairs? They do not have to worry about it if they used the financial institution's power of attorney form. Do you see what I mean? Power of attorney documents come with your newly drafted Revocable Living Trust. You can still use the durable power of attorney documents that come with Revocable Living Trusts but be prepared for some push back. Every financial institution is different and has its processes and acceptance policy. Further, there are differences between states, too. You will likely need a letter of incapacity from a physician. Go get that **before** you go to the bank to make yourself a power of attorney on your parent's account(s).

I do not even want to assume that you have no will or trust set up. That would be worse than Joe Biden at the teleprompter.

Everyone should have a Revocable Living Trust, even young people. There are several financial planning and advisor networks with attorneys who agree to discount their fees in drafting Revocable Living Trusts and ancillary documents (i.e., DPOA's, Health Care POA's, Living Wills, etc.) I am affiliated with one of these financial planning and advisor networks, specifically Estate Plan Navigator: https://www.epnavigator.com. Vanilla is another one that is popular among financial planners and advisors. It is located at https://www.justvanilla.com. I may use them at some point. All I have to do is sign up. There are significantly more bells and whistles in the way of specialized reporting and checklists with Vanilla that may appeal to you. I chose Estate Plan Navigator because their documents are **drafted and reviewed by attorneys**. Heliosplans is another one and they are located at https://heliosplans.com.

I am sure that you know that several online firms offer Revocable Living Trusts that attorneys do not review. They just spit out the documents and charge a small fee. I have already seen mistakes in one of these firms by not knowing Florida law. Florida requires two witnesses *and* a notary, and that was the mistake that I found. It was notarized, but it did not have two witnesses. I am not a fan of these online companies because the documents I have seen are too basic. I like to cover all the contingencies. Things like an Intent to Return where even if you are in a nursing home, your intention is to return to your home at some point. Most boilerplate documents do not have these kind of forms.

I believe in the services of an attorney, and in these financial planning and advisor networks, you can find them for as low as $1,000 to around $1,500. In addition, they can do joint trusts for couples within the same fee range. However, you need to factor in your situation as a couple regarding whether you need two single trusts or one joint trust. If your relationship is on shaky ground, you may want to have separate trusts. Everyone is different.

Once you create a Revocable Living Trust, then you need to re-title assets in the name of this new trust. People often make the mistake of naming their trust like this:

"John and Jane Doe Revocable Living Trust"

Instead, they should not include their name in the trust for a little bit of privacy. Some examples of alternative naming would be J&J D

Revocable Trust, Doe Family Revocable Trust, or two-family names like the last name and the spouse's maiden name. For example, you could name it Doe-Smith Revocable Trust. I have clients who name their trusts after cities or animals and do not include their names. There is no hard and fast rule regarding Revocable Living Trust naming strategies. Think about real estate titling, for example. You may be able to keep things a little private with your Revocable Living Trust naming methods. You will still have to prove you are the trustee when retitling accounts, but some privacy is offered with trust naming strategies when people look up your publicly available real estate record online. Who is going to know what the Wolf Revocable Trust is? They may think your last name is Wolf, but it is not. You named it that because you like wolves. Unique naming strategies provide a little bit of privacy, as you can see.

Nobody likes to talk about death or think about prearranging your funeral. However, it is one of the best things you can do for yourself and your family. Your spouse, son, or daughter does not want to make these decisions for you, especially when grieving. Most funeral homes have payment plans or insurance policies that you can pay over time.

Unfortunately, there are many families with adult children who cannot wait until your demise. I learned about a recent case where both parents have dementia. These people are not my clients. I heard about it from a CPA, so some gossip is involved, but I think the story is mostly accurate. One spouse was utterly helpless with full-blown dementia, and the other has been diagnosed with early-onset dementia, so neither one is capable of taking care of themselves. They have four adult children. Right now, the adult children (and their spouses) were spending a week at a time taking care of mom and dad. Mom and dad own a $350,000 house jointly, and they have about $50,000 in the bank, plus social security and a small pension. One of the adult children's spouse was over at mom and dad's house and got mom to sign a check to her without any of the other sibling's knowledge. Luckily, the bank did not cash the check because they knew about their mom's situation. However, these types of cases happen more often than you think. The problem with this scenario is that the adult children and their spouses have jobs and cannot continue this once per week routine. One of them lives out of state and drives two hours each way for their volunteer week. How long can this continue?

Equally unfortunate is that these adult children think that they will get their hands on this $50,000 and the house. I recommended an elder law attorney to the CPA and told him (a male) that it might cost them $15,000. The CPA passed on my explanation as best he could but got nowhere with them. They immediately balked at the thought of paying an attorney $15,000. They do not realize that their parents, both of them, need to qualify for Medicaid and enter a nursing home. One of them needs to gain acceptance to a nursing home right now. Oh, I'm sorry. Did you think you can just walk straight into any nursing home? Most have waiting lists, and they will take those who can pay over Medicaid for their semi-private rooms. There are no private rooms with Medicaid.

You cannot qualify for Medicaid until you are down to $2,000 and **assign all your income** to the nursing home. They are not going to get that $50,000. They cannot gift it away because Medicaid looks back **<u>five years</u>** and demands payment before they approve their admission to any nursing home. I tried to explain that they can either pay the elder law attorney the $15,000 to preserve as much as possible, or do nothing, and pay the nursing homeowner the $15,000. **It is as simple as that.** The nursing homeowner cannot help them, whereas <u>the elder law attorney can help them</u>. The adult children foolishly believe that they ***<u>will not</u>*** have to pay either the attorney **<u>or</u>** the nursing home owner. As Donald Trump used to say during a debate, "Wrong!" I have this same conversation repeatedly, but people have a hard time fully understanding this (impending doom) and get stuck on the fee to the attorney. Especially when they have never hired an attorney in their life. You may not like injury attorneys blasting ads on television all the time, but elder law attorneys usually are very caring and compassionate people. Think about it. They are in the business of helping the elderly. What is nobler than that?

In my example, the four adult children and their spouses have chosen to continue with their once-a-week rotation. However, what happens when one of their small company employers says, no more? "You have to work and be here. We cannot allow you to take off what essentially is a whole quarter of the year to care for aging parents." What happens then? Sadly, they chose the wrong road. Yes, there is the Family Medical Leave Act, but that does not pay the bills. FMLA is <u>unpaid</u> and only guarantees your health insurance and job back. There is an approval process to qualify for FMLA, too. FMLA typically allows for **12** weeks off per year unless you are military (26 weeks), and **you have to work for a company with more than <u>50</u> employees**. It **<u>is not</u>** available if the adult children work for a small employer. Here is a link to an FMLA PowerPoint presentation on the DOL's website. https://www.dol.gov/agencies/whd/fmla/general-guidance Click the link for "Family and Medical Leave Act (Microsoft PowerPoint)."

The elder law attorney does complex elder care planning for people in the above situation and worse! They do not realize that the elder law attorney knows all the Medicaid-eligible nursing homes in the area. Are you going to get in the car and drive all over town hunting down the best nursing home? What are your qualifications to do this type of search? What if they do not have any open beds available? The elder law attorney knows how to fill out the forms and get your parent(s) qualified for Medicaid and <u>*admitted*</u>!

Another professional who may help you get your parent(s) qualified for Medicaid is someone who does the Medicaid application process for a fee. There are few and far between of these Medicaid professionals, so you have to look hard to find them. Further, you have to pay them, too. Keep in mind that they can do nothing for you to preserve assets. Only the elder law attorney can help you preserve assets. These Medicaid professionals will tell you the same thing that I described above. You have to assign all of your income to the nursing home and pay them that $50,000 before Medicaid pays a cent.

There are other possibilities of helping out with nursing home costs if your parent is a Veteran or widowed spouse of a Veteran who served at least one day of active duty during wartime. However, their **income and assets** have to be less than roughly $130,000 in total to qualify for the benefit. That $130,000 limitation knocks out most people based on that alone. Also, please understand that even if your parent(s) did qualify, then guess where the money goes? It goes to the nursing home!

These adult children do not realize that they have to pay the nursing home with any available income (social security and pensions) before Medicaid will pay a penny.

> <u>All their income</u> goes to the nursing home when you are on Medicaid.

There is no way around that fact. As I said, you can pay the elder law attorney who can help you and try to save as much of your estate as possible, or you can be very foolish and pay the nursing homeowner. That is your choice. Otherwise, be prepared to add a whole lot of stress to your life.

The elder law attorney knows trust strategies like saving some of the money with trusts and pre-paying funeral expenses or buying burial plots or insurance. In some states, when the house is sold after death and Medicaid has been paying for both spouses' nursing home care for several years combined, **Medicaid can go after the house proceeds to repay <u>with a lien</u>**. Did you know that? These adult children will not get the entire proceeds from the sale of the house either. They may not get any of it with two parents in a nursing home. That is too bad. This failure is due to a lack of elder care planning and not hiring an elder law attorney early on. Will this be you? Or will you be brilliant and plan for this contingency?

This is worth repeating. Typically, from an income perspective, you have to sign over your social security and pensions to pay the cost of the nursing home. **You cannot keep them**. The nursing homeowner gets paid regardless of whether your income covers it or not. You have to have Medicaid fill in the gaps. Medicaid does not pay a penny if there is enough social security and pension income to cover the cost of the nursing home or if you have made any gifts within the last five (5) years. It is when there is a shortfall between mom and dad's income that Medicaid will step in. By the way, I hope there is no mortgage on their house. Who will pay the mortgage when all mom and dad's income pay the nursing home costs?

You may be wondering about assisted living centers instead of nursing homes. Here is what usually happens. People go into the assisted living center that has a nursing home attached. They may go in paying $3,000 per month, but as soon as they need more round-the-clock care, then that bumps up to around $6,000 per month. Do you see why the nursing homeowner is happy and prosperous? Their income doubles when someone goes from assisted living to his nursing home. I wonder.

> "Does the nursing homeowner have a slight conflict of interest to tell you that your parent needs round-the-clock care sooner rather than later? You tell me."

When there are two spouses with dementia, then the costs are double. Their social security and pension income will not cover all the costs, especially when you are talking about around **$12,000 per month for two parents who need round-the-clock care.** Therefore, Medicaid will most likely be required. The $50,000 that the adult children in my story believe they are going to inherit, instead will be going to the nursing homeowner, and **it has to whether they want it**

to or not. In addition, if they are foolish enough to pay themselves the $50,000 to hide it, then Medicaid will refuse to pay the first $50,000 to the nursing home. Did you know that? Further, Medicaid will stop the presses and look for other money transfers within the last five years.

> Medicaid *requires* bank statements and investment account statements as part of its application process. You cannot hide anything from Medicaid. They are friends with the IRS.

Think about that. What if the adult children took the money, then spent it? That is when they will get the shock that mom and dad cannot get into the nursing home until they pay back that $50,000? Well, they spent it, so they cannot pay it back. Their poor parents are screwed. If they die after that, who will pay the funeral expenses when the adult children ran off with all the money? They will need to keep doing their weekly rotation because they were so selfish and did not do what was in their parents' best interest. These adult children are probably not getting the house's total value, either. They are certainly not receiving their social security and pension income. That will disappear like a camera operator at Joe Biden's southern border with Mexico. Poof!

Oh, did I mention that Medicaid can also claw back charitable gifts? Even innocuous gifts of $1,000 here and there can be clawed back. You **cannot** give away money to anyone or any organization (even church) without Medicaid looking back for five years to claw it back. This begs the question, "Should you have a five-year plan to protect assets from Medicaid clawbacks or wait until a crisis hits and be in a worse scenario?" This is why **pre-paying** the elder law attorney far in advance of your death might be a good idea, especially if you have assets to protect. I know some elder law attorneys who charge significantly less than $15,000 to those who pre-plan in advance.

I wanted to discuss another thing regarding Medicaid. If you have IRAs that have required minimum distributions (RMD's), in some states, they will let you keep the IRA principal but take the RMD's every year to apply towards your nursing home or LTC costs. Other states **will make you liquidate your IRA** to pay the nursing home or LTC costs **before they will pay a cent**. By the way, you have to pay taxes on your entire IRA when you liquidate them. All in one year! Did you know that about having to liquidate your IRA because of Medicaid qualifying? That's what I thought! You may want to do an online search to determine whether Medicaid **in your state** makes you liquidate your IRA. I would imagine that you would agree with me that this fact is vital to know. Medicaid is a federal program, but the states run it. Each state has its own Medicaid rules. Now you see another reason why people are moving to Florida. You can keep your IRA principal. At least that was the case the last time that I checked.

Hopefully, you can see why there is simply no way to "do it yourself." The elder law attorney is the only person on the planet that can give you any sense of hope in this situation. The best decision you can ever make is to hire an elder law attorney and pay them because they are worth every cent. The only thing these adult children can hope for is that both parents die and die soon. That is not a good alternative. Typically, you can count on a person with dementia living between two to ten years, depending on the type and the age first diagnosed. As of today, you may need $6,000 per month per parent. Do they have that kind of income? If not, you need an elder law attorney to plan for contingencies. Or should I say emergencies?

I wanted to shift gears slightly and talk about account titling issues. It is better to have a conversation with your parent(s) about all of their investment and insurance accounts **before** they get to the point of mental incapacity. You should immediately do a **beneficiary check** on any insurance accounts (life or annuity policies) and all IRAs, Roth IRAs, 401(k)s, and any other type of retirement plan. All of these account types will have a beneficiary or should. You may find that a deceased person is listed as the beneficiary like a former spouse, for example, and needs to be rectified. For those who have a Revocable

Living Trust, then it makes things very easy. All you do is put down the Revocable Living Trust as the beneficiary unless you have specific bequests to particular beneficiaries. If you do name your trust as the beneficiary, things will go according to the trust terms.

Individual and joint accounts do not have beneficiaries unless you add a **transfer on death** (payable on death) clause to them. Most people do not use this feature on individual and joint accounts, but it is simply filling out a form. If you do that, then all the accounts will have their beneficiaries reviewed (and corrected if necessary) to comply with the individual's wishes as described in their Revocable Living Trust.

You would not believe the amount of work that goes into figuring out your account beneficiaries. Nor do you realize the amount of work it takes to re-title all of your accounts in the name of your Revocable Living Trust, especially if there are several accounts. I routinely see people with over 20 accounts. Re-titling accounts is a long process that can take months sometimes, so it is best not to delay. Forms have to be mailed and notarized a lot of times. You may have to visit banks, insurance agents, and financial advisor offices, which can take time. It is best to get things buttoned up sooner rather than later.

You may be wondering about long-term care insurance. Regular long-term care (LTC) insurance is costly. LTC insurance is guaranteed renewable, but they can raise the premiums every single year, and trust me, they do. Most people cannot afford this type of LTC insurance, nor can they easily qualify for it medically. This type of LTC insurance has stringent underwriting for policy issuance. Sometimes, even if you have the money to buy it, you still may not be able to qualify for it.

The other type of LTC insurance sold by insurance agents is the **Hybrid LTC** policy. A Hybrid LTC policy is essentially a **single premium life insurance policy** with an **LTC rider**. However, it is medically underwritten, which means if you cannot pass the medical underwriting guidelines, then the Hybrid LTC policy simply becomes an annuity. An annuity? Oh no! We learned about annuities earlier.

We are better off investing the money ourselves. If you are one of the few and far between who can qualify with medical underwriting, then you simply need to do a calculation on whether or not you can beat the Hybrid LTC policy with your investment account. (Duh! You can because you keep your principal!) It will still be an "annuitization like" issue, but if you medically qualify, they may give you a little extra income stream. It essentially works in this manner. Suppose you gave the insurance company $100,000 for a Hybrid LTC policy. If you medically qualify, you may receive a death benefit of $190,000, if you are around 65 years old for example. Then, this $190,000 becomes your pool of money for LTC. Once they pay you the $190,000, which would last perhaps three years, then it is gone—no more benefits once that runs out.

Here is where the insurance agent gets stupid believing those glossy brochures. If you were to buy a Hybrid LTC policy today and qualify for the $190,000, that means you are healthy today. Understand that this $190,000 will grow at the low interest rates currently being offered **based on the original investment of $100,000**. If, on the other hand, you invested $100,000 using the rule of 72, it may double in 8 or 9 years to $200,000 in a diversified or focused portfolio. If you qualified medically, then that means that you will likely live longer than ten years, or they would not have given you that Hybrid LTC policy at $190,000. (By the way, the older you are, the smaller that death benefit or pool of money.) If after 8 or 9 years you have doubled your $100,000 to $200,000, you are in an equal position as the Hybrid LTC policy. If you live for 16 - 18 years before needing LTC, then you will have $400,000 — $500,000 for your pool of money for LTC. (Insurance agents do not get this fact.) With the Hybrid LTC, you will likely have much less than that after the same amount of time because of the low-interest rates offered for Hybrid LTC policies. The kicker is that **you control your own money**! If you buy the Hybrid LTC policy, then the insurance company controls it, and it is gone quicker than Joe

Biden leaving a teleprompter reading. If you cannot qualify medically, then it is essentially worthless because it becomes annuity-like, and there is no reason to give the insurance company your money. It is better that you control it.

As I said, you have to calculate the numbers to see if it is worth it. Their interest rate assumptions are always a bunch of nonsense, meaning they are **not guaranteed**. By the way, this Hybrid LTC policy is intended to pay for LTC costs, so do not assume that it will be paid to beneficiaries. It goes to pay for LTC. (You have to submit claims to the insurance company.) There could be money for beneficiaries if they did not use the Hybrid LTC policy for LTC (i.e., died from an accident or suddenly). In case of an accident or sudden death, then your heirs would receive the death benefit. One more thing that I wanted to point out. Interest crediting rates are low, and as long as they stay down, you can beat it in most cases.

Always keep in mind that insurance companies offer hybrid LTC policies. Who benefits first? The insurance company. Who benefits second? The insurance agent. Who benefits last? **You!**

The insurance company swallows your principal if you need LTC because they are essentially paying you with your principal! Think about it. If your $100,000 grew to $190,000 in 10 years, then what is the insurance company's risk? Not much as I see it. You may be wondering what is your risk? Your risk is only in the early years before you are able to accumulate that $190,000. Once you accumulate the $190,000 with your diversified or focused portfolio, then buying the Hybrid LTC policy is a loser from that point on. Your investment account will continue to grow at a more rapid rate as opposed to the Hybrid LTC policy that pays very low interest rates. Do you see?

Without the medical qualification, it effectively becomes an annuity. Oops! We do not like annuities because all they do is take our principal, leaving nothing for our beneficiaries, and pay us a guaranteed income stream. So what if it is guaranteed? If we control our own money, we can guarantee our income stream! Our investment account is tax-deferred until we sell something if we are buying stocks or ETF's. We can do better with a diversified or focused portfolio if we follow the guidelines in this book.

The insurance agent makes a hefty commission (10% — 15%), and you locked up your money in something with 10 — 15 years of surrender charges that you have no idea, if and when, you will ever need it. Nor do you know how much your death benefit will end up being, if anything. It is all hocus-pocus, in my opinion.

You will probably need some professional help to evaluate these Hybrid LTC policies properly. I would suggest talking to a registered investment adviser to assess a Hybrid LTC policy adequately. Most insurance agents' evaluation consists of showing you a brochure, whereas a registered investment adviser has calculation tools to evaluate a Hybrid LTC policy properly. A simple Excel® or Numbers® spreadsheet will help you. All you do is take the illustration for the Hybrid LTC policy and enter that into your spreadsheet. You need to have multiple columns for both the guaranteed and current assumptions. You would have a cash value column and a death benefit or LTC pool of funds column for each assumption. Once you enter that into your spreadsheet, make an interest rate assumption for your diversified portfolio and your focused portfolio (i.e., 7 — 9%). Project that out the same number of years as your Hybrid LTC illustration. You should find out that after 10 — 14 years, keeping your own money is the best choice. If you are medically qualified for the Hybrid LTC policy, it is not too much of a stretch for you to live that long. You qualified for it, therefore the actuarial odds of you living 10 — 14 years is fairly good.

You may be asking yourself, **"What if I do not want to pay for my LTC?"** Now you are asking about **asset protection** strategies. Putting it another way, "How do I protect my assets from seizure by Medicaid in case I need LTC?" It is simple. You need an elder law attorney to draft an irrevocable trust for taxable assets that you intend to give away to heirs and **start a five-year clock** on those assets. Gift the assets to the trust while you are still healthy, and once the five years have elapsed, your assets are free from seizure by Medicaid and other creditors. This is true because, by creating an irrevocable trust, you have essentially given those assets away. Technically, they are no longer yours. If you die, they go where you wanted them to go anyway. The attorney can draft the irrevocable trust so you can receive, or your spouse can receive income from it. The trustee can withhold income once the need to qualify for Medicaid happens.

To fully understand this issue, I want you to assume that you are **single** and have $500,000, and you were taking income of 4% or $20,000 per year from it. If it is not in an irrevocable trust and instead in a non-qualified (taxable) account, you would have to spend that $500,000 on your long-term care before you could ever qualify for Medicaid. If, on the other hand, you had set up an irrevocable trust at least five years earlier and then put that same $500,000 in it while healthy and took the same 4% per year from it, then you could essentially turn off the income. Medicaid has no recourse because you do not own that $500,000 anymore. The trustee no longer has to pay you any income, which is good because you want to qualify for Medicaid now. You gave it away when you deposited it into the irrevocable trust over five years ago. This example is how elder law attorneys protect assets by starting the five-year clock and utilizing irrevocable trusts.

Further asset protection is possible with **multiple irrevocable trusts**. Put your life insurance policy in an irrevocable life insurance trust and start a five-year clock on that trust. Medicaid does not allow you to have cash value life insurance, except for final expense life insurance which is usually $15,000 in death benefit or less. If you have $25,000 in cash value in a life policy, then guess what? Medicaid makes you liquidate that and use it towards your long term care costs.

Without utilizing an elder law attorney, that death benefit that you thought you were leaving to your adult children or spouse will go by the wayside.

You can establish other irrevocable trusts for other property like multiple real estate properties. You can make your business have an irrevocable trust, but I would have the elder law attorney advise you on that issue for sure. Each state has specific laws related to companies owned by trusts. You need to hire an elder law attorney to do it right. There are lots of creative things you can do to protect family assets. Things get a little trickier when you are married and have IRAs. If one spouse needs LTC and the other spouse does not, then the spouse who does not can only have between $2,155.00 (minimum) and $3,259.50 (maximum) per month in income according to Medicaid. That is relatively consistent across all states, with a few exceptions. That is not enough for one spouse to live on, obviously, so this is why you need the elder law attorney. Further, you do not want a surviving spouse to inherit (take receipt of) money from a Revocable Living Trust that has become irrevocable. If that Revocable Living Trust was properly drafted by an elder law attorney, then the income stream from this now irrevocable trust can be turned off in order for the surviving spouse to qualify for Medicaid. If the surviving spouse takes receipt of the funds, then they lose this asset protection and have to use that money for their own elder care expenses. I am telling you. Elder law attorneys are your friend!

Further, it depends on the state you live in and whether or not you have to liquidate your IRA. The elder law attorney can help you with the more complex aspects of this type of asset protection planning. If you do not do anything, <u>you will be spending your own money on your LTC</u> if you find yourself in that predicament. That may be okay with you, but at least now you know things to consider.

Unfortunately, you cannot do asset protection yourself. You <u>will not</u> find irrevocable trusts online that you can buy on the cheap.

Hopefully, I scared you into action concerning your situation or your parent's situation. **Plan ahead please!** It will make a ton of difference if you do. Do not be one of those people who do nothing. I know a young lady in this predicament. Her father died, and he had not done a thing! She had to have a Go Fund Me account set up to help pay her father's funeral costs. That is ridiculous. Do not let this happen to your son or daughter.

CHAPTER THIRTY-FIVE
A Final Word

The PINO administration recently "took over," as evidenced by the fencing, barbed wire, and National Guard in Washington, DC (but "there is no evidence of election fraud"). I suspect that you may have noticed a spike in gas prices with a threat of a further increase in gas or miles-driven taxes that affects everyone. In addition, you may have seen the loss of Keystone pipeline jobs, a halt to the border wall, and a crisis in illegal immigration as a result. The Palestinians are back firing rockets at Israel after the PINO administration gave the Palestinians over $200,000,000 recently. They bought the rockets from Iran no less. Iran sees weakness in the PINO administration, and they are exploiting it. Further still, you may have heard talk about raising corporate taxes. I never received a job from a poor person. How about you? Raising corporate taxes means less jobs and higher prices to consumers.

Who in their right mind would ever vote to raise their taxes? No one in their right mind. Only people in their left mind. You can thank the PINO for this disastrous nightmare. The PINO administration did this on purpose, by the way, and if you voted for this, then you get what you deserve. Sorry, but I am telling you the truth, which is something sorely lacking from liberal and progressive politicians these days. I cannot tell you how many times the fake news media and their liberal and progressive friends (Silicon Valley) said, "There is no evidence of election fraud."

Let me do what Jesus would do and use an analogy. What if your investment professional, when you complained about poor performance, said,

> "There is no evidence of poor performance in your portfolio."

Never mind the fact that you are looking at your account statements and have the proof in your hand, otherwise known as "the evidence." When you try to hand your account statements to your investment professional (he is the judge), he says,

> "Nope. Sorry, but I refuse to accept those documents. It is a moot point since that statement is from November 3, 2020."

This is precisely what happened with our election. No evidence was ever presented because of the media, Silicon Valley tech firms, the politicians (right and left), the FBI, the Department of Justice, state courts, federal appeals courts, and the Supreme Court all sided one way — **against the American people**. Sorry, but I am not going to apologize for telling the truth. I looked behind the curtain, and there is no Wizard of Oz. Remember that the National Guard is guarding Washington, DC as I write this, and they put up a fence with barbed wire around the Capitol area! Supposedly, 81 million people voted for Joe Biden, more than any President in American history, even Barrack Obama! If that were true, he should be the most loved President in American history. Is he? Give me a break. Do they need the National Guard? The National Guard is sleeping on the floor of a parking garage, but illegal immigrants are getting to stay in hotels for $86,000,000 of our taxpayer dollars. Does this make any sense at all? Calling out the National Guard is all a political charade to try and paint American Patriots (my readers) as dangerous "domestic terrorists," "white supremacists," and "Uncle Toms."

What about the community organizers of Black Lives Matter, where communities were destroyed and multiple people died, including police officers at their events all last year? I did not see any of their community organizers brought up on charges. Did you? Several of these Democratic cities looked like war zones after BLM events. Nothing happened to any of those BLM community organizers. Have you ever read what BLM stands for? Go to their website and read it. It is complete lunacy. Oh by the way, did you hear about one of the founders of BLM has bought some very expensive homes? It is always about the money. BLM raises money, the organizers enrich themselves on the backs of people with "white guilt" and they in turn donate it to the Democrats. It is a pretty shrewd strategy on BLM's part if you think about it. The "white guilt" people who fell for it are dumb as a fence post, in my opinion.

For fear of being called racists, corporate America lined up to donate money to BLM. Most Democratic governors and mayors stood idly by as their cities were destroyed. They did nothing because they wanted to advance a political agenda. Portland, Oregon, is still ablaze as I write this.

Anyone with a lick of sense knows what is going on. It is an attempt to destroy people who believe in the US Constitution and free and fair elections. They want to make sure that the swamp is left alone, and if anyone tries to come along and eliminate the swamp, then this is what they can expect. It is as simple as that. Rush Limbaugh explained this over and over again on the EIB network. The Democrats succeeded in the 2020 election, but will they in future elections? That is up to you. **You cannot ever again take your vote for granted.** This fight is about saving our country as founded. Do not despair. Do not give up and fail to vote. You should vote for conservative principles in every election going forward. Stand up. Speak up. Attend pro-conservative events, but I want you to scrutinize your political donations. Do not just hand over your money to a political action committee on a whim. Do your homework!

American Patriots are sick of this "woke" bull crap from CEO's. If you are the CEO of a major corporation, then why on earth would you do something to alienate your customers? It is not your job to be a "woke" champion for cancel culture (fascism). I can tell you one thing. <u>American Patriots will never forget</u> which companies are "woke," and they will vote with their wallets and pocketbooks. As a CEO of a major corporation, I cannot believe that you thought it was a good idea to alienate your investors and customers! How dumb is that? I think the damage has already been done. We will see changes in CEOs before you know it. The pendulum always swings back to the middle.

Our sports leaders are worse. They are the biggest chicken sh*ts on the planet. They are so scared about upsetting their players that they side with them instead of their fans. Is this not the dumbest thing ever? Get a clue. The fans pay for everything! If you tick off your fans, then guess what? They may not spend any more money on your sport! Duh! That is called "freedom," by the way. These sports leaders sorely lack advisers with a spine who would have nixed their "woke" thinking before making those dumb decisions. Time will tell, but I would not bet against an American Patriot. I believe these sports leaders will live to regret their ignorant decisions. Look at the NBA ratings. They are in the proverbial toilet.

Although we have watched as our political power has been diminished in the short term, I believe that we will turn it around in the 2022 election and beyond. The Democrats have overplayed their hand. **This "woke" nightmare is only temporary**. Whenever liberals and progressives get in power, they screw things up like "Hogan's goat." They are well on their way as I write this to screwing everything up. If a small percentage of the people on the left realize that they have been had by the lying Democratic politicians, we can swing it to our side. Democrats make promises that they have no intention of keeping.

They only say those things to get elected. Conservatives are not stupid enough to fall for those false promises.

Ask a Keystone pipeline worker how they feel after having voted for the PINO. Or a Ford factory worker who thought their factory job was safe but learned that their job is going to Mexico again! Further, still, ask a black person if they feel safe in their Democratically run city. In addition to that, ask an inner-city black parent if they worry about their child getting accidentally shot and killed. It happens in Democrat-run cities every week, but the Democrats do not care about black people. Democrats are the biggest racists out there. They do not want to help black people have a better life. They only want to keep black people in crappy schools run by teachers' unions, on the government dole, and beholden to them for votes. **It is that simple**. If you are black, then you need to quit letting these liberal and progressive politicians keep you in this box. You need to break free of their control. As Donald J. Trump said, "What do you have to lose?" By the way, the lowest black unemployment rate was achieved under President Trump. This is why they wanted to get rid of him. If President Trump was re-elected (and he was), then the Democrats could not allow black people to realize that they can have a better life than the one offered by liberals and progressives. The Democrats cannot have black people doing well for themselves. Otherwise, they would lose their stranglehold over their voters. If you are black, according to the Democrats, you have to stay on the Democrat's "plantation." Wake the hell up! Democrats are the racists! The truth is right in front of you. Think critically! You do not have to be smart to figure this out. Do you have school choice? Has BLM helped you personally? Has crime gone down in your inner-city neighborhood? What has a Democrat done to help you get ahead in life? What job opportunities and training in high-skilled jobs have the Democrats provided to you? The answer to all those questions is no, or nothing at all. Who are the real racists? You tell me.

The PINO administration has opened our border to illegal immigrants to build up a base of people beholden to the government and who will keep the Democrats in power for a long time. The Democrats are making a mistake. Most of these illegal immigrants are Catholic and believe in Christianity. It is not a lock that they will all vote Democrat in the future. I doubt the Democrats will win over as many of these people as they think, even if they grant them all amnesty. American Patriots will stop it by explaining what being a Democrat means to their Hispanic friends. You will not hear much talk about freedom of religion from a Democrat. They want to take God out of everything. If you are an American Patriot, you need to explain to your Hispanic friends the truth every chance you get. Plus, your white friends are the real problem. They are the ones voting Democrat out of "white guilt," I suppose. Nothing else makes any sense. They can never give a coherent argument as to why they vote Democrat because they do not stand for anything. Conservatives are American Patriots, and we have values and stances that we believe in and can explain without reservation. Democrats go into accusation mode when they cannot explain their positions. It is like the philosopher Socrates asking people who thought they believed in something to explain it to him. Socrates simply asked question after question until the person who thought they were so smart and sure of themselves ended up walking away in embarrassment. That is today's Democrat.

We conservatives have the power to vote in good people who have conservative principles and, more importantly, who adhere to them. This is our main power over Washington, DC, and we must wield it. **Get rid of the RINOs!** Vote every RINO out of office when you have the opportunity to replace them with a conservative.

May God bless you and your family. May God bless our great country, the United States of America. Thank you for being an American Patriot and one of my valued readers. In addition, I would appreciate it if you told your friends, family, and co-workers about this book. I cannot help everybody, but I can help my American Patriot readers.

CHAPTER THIRTY-SIX

About the Author

Richard Mark Allison

Rick was born in Little Rock, Arkansas, in 1956. His parents, Bill and Donna, divorced before his first birthday. Both Bill and Donna remarried, and Rick grew up with his mother and her new husband at the time, Hillman E. Johnson. Hillman and Donna had three children, Sharri, David, and Gary. Bill remarried and also had three children, Tami, Jon and Kelly.

Hillman was in the life insurance business, and in 1984, Rick obtained his life insurance license to learn the business from Hillman Johnson. Hillman was 6'6" tall with a commanding presence. He was well-loved by his friends and clients. Hillman was quite a character and very funny. Hillman always had a nickname for his friends. Ricardo Montalbán and Hollywood were my two nicknames.

After working as essentially an apprentice insurance agent under Hillman, I noticed that people were more eager to discuss their investment portfolio than they were their life insurance needs. Since Hillman was not licensed for securities, I decided that we could feed off each other with me handling investments for his life agency. Thus began my quest to learn how to design investment portfolios (for American Patriots).

In 1988, I obtained my Series 7 license. At first, I went to one of those Series 7 boot camp kind of places but realized that people running the boot camp had no interest in anything other than collecting my fee, so I dropped out and studied for the Series 7 on my own. I passed on my first attempt. People around me told me that the

Series 63 was a piece of cake if you already passed the Series 7, so I took that bad advice and did not study for five minutes for it. Of course, I promptly bombed it with a 67 when I needed a 70 to pass. As a result of that 67, I told myself that I would never let that happen again. That failure on a test was something that became etched in my mind for my entire life. I would over-study from that point forward. I ended up with the Series 7, 9, 10, 24, 63, and 65 licenses. Those are all the licenses that you must have if you work in the broker-dealer world as a branch manager. With those licenses, I was a branch manager for a couple of regional broker-dealers and also I was a branch manager for a national broker-dealer, Charles Schwab & Co., Inc. in Jacksonville, FL.

In 1990, I began a quest for my Certified Financial Planner® Designation. I took six courses from the College for Financial Planning in Denver, Colorado. These were all self-study courses, which is how I preferred it. I passed each of those six courses in succession and earned my CFP® designation on December 1, 1992. My CFP® license number is 045467, in case you want to look me up at https://cfp.net.

After passing the CFP®, I studied for the Chartered Mutual Fund Counselor® designation. I completed this in 1998. In 2005, I completed the Chartered Advisor for Senior Living® designation, and as a glutton for punishment, I obtained my real estate sales associate license in 2006.

I never again failed an exam for all of those licenses described above. My secret was to always over-study. After reading the *Foreword* to this book, then you will recall that I earned my BA in Criminal Justice from UA-Little Rock at age 60. My wife calls me a professional student. Here we were from our church directory picture a few years ago. Natalie and I were married in 1988. She is an incredible person who likes to do things for other people. I married way over my head, let me tell you.

Although affiliated with different firms for most of my career, I maintained my level of independence. For whatever reason, I like working with people smarter than me, who can mentor me and teach me new ideas. When that dried up, then I moved on. Since October 1, 2008, I have been at Marian Financial Services, Inc., where I am today. I own the firm lock, stock, and barrel. My website is located at: https://marianfs.com. In addition, I own another company, RIA Rules, LLC, that offers compliance consulting to smaller registered investment adviser firms. My RIA Rules, LLC website is located at: https://riarules.com.

My interests include playing baseball. I have played in the Men's Senior Baseball League since I was 32 years old. I still play in it. Instead of playing in the 30+ division, I am now in the 60+ division! Be honest. How many 60+-year-old people do you know that play baseball? That's what I thought! Here is a picture of me and some of my closest friends from Arkansas. L to R: Gregg Rollins (catcher), Jimmy Scott (a pitcher), Rick Allison (outfielder), and Randall Guard (a pitcher).

The following picture is of my son and daughter, Marshall and Rudi, taken at her graduation from the University of Central Florida. Marshall went to Florida State University. We are very blessed to have such beautiful children who are now adults. Time passes fast, my friends.

This book is my fifth book. The previous four books were written under my former name Richard Allison Johnson. If I had to grade myself on those four books, I would be pretty harsh, except the prior one, Meet Wally Street. The Reason You're Stupid, 2nd edition. I added many pictures in the 2nd edition, cleaned up some minor errors, and added some new information. However, that book is now seven (7)

years old, so I would not recommend that you buy it. I am just honest about it. Do not waste your money unless you are a glutton for punishment. This book will not be my last book. I am already working on a fiction book. I need to put my criminal justice degree to use. I am leaning towards a book about a group of guys who go after stalkers. I hate those stalker creeps. It will be a crime novel! Watch for it!

You may be wondering about my name change. I simply changed my name back to the name that I was born with, Richard Mark Allison. I was never adopted or anything. My mom simply changed my name to match my Johnson siblings, which I can understand, but I did not have to like it. I can remember the day she told me in first grade. I was mad, and boy was I mad. I never did like it after she did it. After decades of thinking about changing it, I finally decided to do it. I cannot tell you how happy this has made me. I feel like the universe has been appropriately re-aligned. I think you would agree after you read about my Allison genealogy in the *Foreward* section. I am proud to be an Allison with such a storied history.

As you can see from all the licenses and exams that I have taken, you can quickly see how I could write this book. I have all those previously described professional experiences under my belt, so writing this book was easy. The editing part is always the toughest. You think you are finished, then you find another error, or you find the need to add another sentence or two. You keep re-reading it and find yet another mistake and yet another one. This editing process continues for weeks until you finally reach the end.

THE END

About the Author

Richard M. Allison resides in the Northeast Florida area. He is originally from Little Rock, Arkansas where he graduated from the University of Arkansas at Little Rock with a BA in Criminal Justice and a Personal Finance Minor. Rick is a Chartered Advisor for Senior Living®, a Chartered Mutual Fund Counselor® and has been a Certified Financial Planner® since 1992.

His professional experience spans over 33 years and includes roles as a Chief Compliance Officer, Charles Schwab Branch Manager II, Investment Adviser Representative and Insurance Agent.

Richard is the author of five books, four of them under the name of Richard Allison Johnson. Designing an Investment Portfolio for American Patriots® is the culmination of his experiences advising clients over his career.

Mr. Allison's main business is Marian Financial Services, Inc., a registered investment adviser since 2006.

Allison's other business is RIA Rules, LLC where he advises registered investment adviser firms about compliance issues.

Read more at https://marianfs.com.

About the Publisher

RIA Rules, LLC is a Florida LLC.

www.ingramcontent.com/pod-product-compliance
Lightning Source LLC
LaVergne TN
LVHW090401210926
848480LV00002B/416
* 9 7 9 8 2 0 1 5 7 9 0 2 9 *